Job Search Strategy

for College Grads

Job Search Strategy for College Grads

The 10-step plan for career success

By Susan Bernard and Gretchen Thompson

BOB ADAMS INC.
Boston, Massachusetts

Published by Bob Adams Inc.
840 Summer Street
South Boston MA 02127

Graphic illustrations by John Caswell.

Manufactured in the United States of America.

Dedication

To my parents, Marjorie and Berny Schwartz, who taught me the two most important skills in life: how to laugh, and how to dream.

To my husband, Bernard Rotondo, for believing in me.
-Susan Bernard

To my son, Christopher, who is still a great kid in spite of all the hours he lost while I completed this project.

To my mother, Therese Daubenthaler, who dared to dream and shared that dream with me.
-Gretchen Thompson

TABLE OF CONTENTS

Chapter 1:   Narrow your choices!   15
- *Why your first career choice may not be your last.*
- *The specter of "career floundering" and why it shouldn't worry you.*
- *Combat stories: five people tell how they did everything wrong and got the jobs they wanted, and why you can do better.*

Chapter 2:   Target your career!   23
- *Know thyself: who are you; what do you want to do; where do you want to do it?*
- *Why people who have jobs can't remember looking for them.*
- *Never apologize for your degree.*
- *How a summer job as a cook demonstrates your executive potential.*
- *How a taste for wine can lead to a flourishing career.*

Chapter 3:   Do your homework!   35
- *What to look for and where to find it.*
- *How to use your college research skills in your career search.*
- *Knowledge is power: how good research will distinguish you from the pack.*

Chapter 4:   Investigate first-hand!   43
- *Information sleuthing: interviewing for answers.*
- *If you want to find out what it's like to be a horse, ask a horse.*
- *What to ask and how to ask it.*

Chapter 5:   Beef up your resume!   61
- *What employers look for in a resume.*
- *What to include and what to leave out.*
- *Education or experience: which should you stress?*
- *Why colored paper is no substitute for well-framed accomplishments.*

Chapter 6: Personalize your cover letter!   **89**
- *Why the "blind resume" never sees the light of day.*
- *Grabbing the employer's attention: what to put in the cover letter that isn't in the resume.*
- *Tailoring your letter and the importance of letting them know you've done your homework.*

Chapter 7: Use your connections!   **99**
- *How do most college grads find jobs?*
- *Traditional job sources and what to expect from them.*
- *Taking advantage of friends and family: how to use personal contacts as job sources.*

Chapter 8: Initiate direct contacts!   **117**
- *How to take the active approach in job-hunting.*
- *Personnel offices, "the screen", and how to get around them.*
- *How to identify decision-makers and get them to speak with you.*
- *What to say to get an interview.*

Chapter 9: Interview enthusiastically!   **135**
- *What employers expect from you in an interview.*
- *What you can expect from employers in an interview.*
- *Interview dos and don'ts, and the most common interview stumbling blocks.*
- *Preparation and how to "star" in the interview.*

Chapter 10: Evaluate your offers!   **161**
- *How to survive the job search.*
- *Dealing with success; coping with rejection.*
- *Keeping the wheels spinning and yourself in gear.*

Bibliography   **173**

INTRODUCTION

There are dozens of books on the job search. A random sampling at any bookstore will turn up at least five to ten books, making it difficult for the job-hunting novice to know which book to choose. So the first question you will probably ask yourself is, "Why should I read *this* book? How does it differ from other books on the subject?"

WHY YOU SHOULD READ THIS BOOK

● *This book offers a strategy for getting a job.*

Whether you have already begun your job search or are just beginning to think about it, you will quickly realize how difficult it is to develop a job search strategy. Should you start out by writing your resume, or should you take some vocational tests? Do you need to target a career first, or is it better to go on some interviews before making a decision? Should you begin reading want-ads on a daily basis, or are they a waste of time? In short, what is the most effective job search strategy?

Strategy is what this book is all about. It offers a logical and systematic approach to a complex subject. There are no lengthy exercises to complete. There are no hidden secrets to share with you. What you *will* get is a 10-step *strategy* for success.

● *This book is geared specifically for college graduates.*

This is not a book for everyone. It is not for re-entry women, mid-life career changers, high school graduates, or older workers. It could be; the strategy is similar. But the advice and information in this book is specifically geared toward college graduates: soon-to-be graduates, recent graduates, and graduates one to five years out of college.

Job-hunting strategy for college graduates differs from other job-hunting strategies because college graduates have different fears, different hopes, different expectations, and different needs than other people in the work force. The resume a college graduate should write is different than that of a re-entry woman. The research that a college graduate is capable of doing is different than that of a high school graduate. The fears a recent college graduate experiences are different than those of a mid-life career changer.

● *This book has been written from the unique perspectives of a job-seeker and a career counselor.*

Most other job-search books are written solely by career specialists. In many cases, that means job-seeking is presented from a narrow perspective. The authors may understand the clinical elements of the job search, but they do not understand the emotional frustrations which may be the most important factor leading to job search failure. They may recommend certain job search strategies, but they have no idea what it is like to utilize those strategies. And they may take for granted a certain knowledge base regarding job sources or job search skills that the average job-seeker does not possess.

In the case of this book, that is not true. Co-author Susan Bernard represents the perspective of the job-seeker. She is a college graduate who has been on more than one hundred job interviews in her career. She has successfully utilized every strategy in this book. She has worked as an editorial assistant in television news, a magazine editor, a marketing manager, and a salesperson.

Co-author Gretchen Thompson, who is currently the Director of Placement and Career Planning at the UCLA Graduate School of Management, represents the perspective of the career specialist. She has counseled students for more than 16 years. She has worked with undergraduates, engineering graduates, law graduates, and now business graduates. She is well-known in career counseling circles, and is a frequent speaker on career-related topics.

WHAT YOU CAN EXPECT

Here is what you will find in this book:

Chapter 1 will tell you how to approach the job search. It will explain why the job search is a process, not an outcome. It will dispel some common fears by demonstrating why the first career you choose is not the one you have to stick with. It will demystify some cherished beliefs when you are introduced to the concept of career floundering. It will put the job search in its proper perspective.

Chapter 2 is about targeting a career. It will tell you *why* you need to know what you want to do, and where you want to do it. It will explain why that step is crucial to your job search success. It will recommend resources for targeting a career. It will force you to make some career decisions.

In chapters 3 and 4, you will discover how to do labor market research. You will learn how to use the library as a source of information on occupations, industries, and companies. You'll find out what the value of an annual report is. The book will analyze the advantages of using people as a resource, and explain how you can accomplish this. When you're finished, you will have the tools to approach the marketplace from a position of knowledge and strength.

Chapters 5 and 6 will teach you how to write a resume and cover letter, two fundamental elements of an effective job search campaign. The book will explore how to present your background so employers will want to meet with you. It will explain the real purpose of these written documents and their importance in the job search.

Chapter 7 will provide you with an invaluable list of traditional job sources. It will not only expand your knowledge of the job sources available to you, but will also tell you how to use them for maximum effectiveness. It will talk about the value of college placement offices, employment agencies, want-ads, and personal contacts, among other sources. It will tell you what works best and why.

In Chapter 8, the authors will recommend an alternative method for approaching the job search — a more direct approach. You will learn a strategy for uncovering your own leads and pursuing them. You will discover how to identify companies that you'd like to approach for employment. This chapter will suggest methods for pursuing them. You will see examples of innovative job search letters. And it will explain techniques for getting your foot in the door when no job listings are advertised.

Chapter 9 covers interviewing. If you have ever asked yourself, "What do employers expect from me? What are they looking for when they ask about my educational background?" Or, "How can I use the interview to my best advantage?" — this chapter provides the answers. In addition, it suggests methods of preparation, offers interviewing guidelines, and recommends ways in which to follow up.

Finally, Chapter 10 is about survival. It discusses methods for dealing with rejection and success. It exposes the differences between successful and unsuccessful job-seekers. It provides a technique for determining career decisions.

HOW TO READ THIS BOOK

We suggest that you take an active approach. Since there are no long exercises to fill out, we would hope that you read the book quickly in order to understand the overall strategy. Once you've finished, you can go back for a second reading. This time, you should carefully read each chapter and do the necessary work, chapter by chapter. The time frame is up to you. If you are currently in school, it may take you a couple of months before you can go on that first field interview. If you're a recent college graduate, you will need to work through it more rapidly. Within two to three weeks, you should begin your field research. Why? Because momentum is important. There's nothing worse than sitting at home with a college degree, bemoaning your lack of employment. The longer you sit, the more difficult it will be to get up.

For all college graduates — no matter what your situation is — if you come upon a stumbling block, find resource people who can help you. The difficulty of using any book, even the most effective one, is that sometimes you will need information or reinforcement that only another person can give you. Prepare for that eventuality from the outset. Realize that it may take you six months to get that first job. If you can't keep yourself motivated for six months, make sure you develop a support group of people who can help motivate you when you need them. If you can't afford to live without income for six months, make sure you get a temporary job that will support you and allow you to go on interviews during the day.

Last of all, as you read this book, remember that there is no one right way of approaching the job search. We have given you a strategy that we know works, but keep in mind that nothing we tell you is gospel. For every rule, there is a deviation. For every deviation, there is a success story. And that is why the job-search is so interesting. You can do everything right and not get hired. You can do everything wrong and get the job. So don't get too self-indulgent about all this, and don't be too hard on yourself. If you treat it too seriously, it can become devastating if you're not successful right away. If you treat it like a game, it can become a real challenge. We know the stakes are high, and we also know that your personal investment may be great. But just remember — life will go on whether you get hired after the first interview or the fifty-first. With that in mind, let's get started.

Susan Bernard
Gretchen Thompson

April 1984

1
Narrow Your Choices

For most of us, the most difficult part of the job-search game is deciding "what I want to be when I grow up." That's because we're convinced that whatever career we pick, we're stuck with it. We're sure there's only one job we were destined for, if we could only identify it. Since most of us can't identify it, we usually react in one of two ways. We either accept a job that is "temporary-but-not-too-taxing" so we can have the time and energy to figure out what we *really* want to do. Or, we accept a career job that has no relationship to what we like doing, because — after a few initial interviews — we're convinced there is no job that contains all the elements we want.

Either way, it's a depressing reality, although it needn't be. In fact, the job search is a process, not an outcome. In fact, we don't need to decide what we want to be when we grow up, because career development is a constantly evolving process. In fact, it is unlikely that the career we start out with upon graduation will be the career we're involved with five years from now. Why is that?

The answer to this question is that, for most recent college graduates, there is an adjustment period when you start working. After all, you're going from an environment characterized by intellectual freedom and growth to an environment that can be quite different. This transition is usually difficult because you don't have a realistic understanding of the working world. Why should you? You've been in school for more than 15 years, and "doing" something, i.e., working, is quite different than studying about it.

When you start working and find that the career you thought you wanted is very different than you had anticipated, or that your goals and values from school may look quite different to you once you're out in the marketplace, it's natural that you will find this adjustment difficult to make. This is particularly true if you're a liberal arts major. Graduates with applied studies degrees usually experience less of an adjustment problem because their academic training has "prepared" them for a job. They generally have had some on-the-job training that's career-related, through summer jobs, internships, and cooperative education experience. In a tight labor market, they may have difficulty finding a job that's satisfying, but they rarely experience the "career floundering" of their less technical contemporaries. So what's a liberal arts graduate to do?

The best advice is that you recognize that "career floundering" exists and is a natural part of the job search process. Characteristically, it is the period of time between graduation from college and initial job satisfaction. It is where you begin finding your niche in the working world. It is where you test which of the skills and abilities that you've developed in college you want to utilize in a working environment. For some, this adaptation is characterized by external change. You accept a number of different short-term positions until you find out what you like doing best. For others, it may involve changing functions within the same environment until you find a job function that interests you. Either way, it's a period of growth and change, whether it lasts for a few months or a few years. The reality is that *all* college graduates experience career floundering to a greater or lesser degree because your college education does not prepare you for a career. The purpose of college, right or wrong, is to *educate* you, not to *train* you. So most graduates, whether they're in sales, marketing, law, or even engineering, spend some phase of their careers learning how to adapt themselves to their working environment.

The greater lesson is that career floundering does not stop once you've achieved initial job satisfaction. In fact, it may exist (to some extent) at many times throughout your professional career. Although many people think they will find a career they love and will live happily ever after, the reality is quite different. If you find all this difficult to believe, that is understandable. Cherished myths die hard. The following interviews with college graduates about their career decision-making experiences should shed some light on the transition from college to career.

Q: How did you decide what career you wanted to pursue after graduation from college?

"It was very difficult for me. I majored in fine arts, studio art, and art history. And for the first eight months after I graduated, I was unemployed. I didn't know what to do. I had some money saved, so I lived on the money I had until I really had to look for a job. I actually didn't look for the first job I got; *it* found me. I was a secretary to a lawyer who was the brother of a friend of mine, who worked in the legal aid office at UCLA. They paid something like $400 a month. I did this for a year-and-a-half.

"Then I went to Europe for six weeks, thinking somewhere in my mind I would get a job there and do something that was related to art. While I was in Europe, a friend of my mother's told her that she'd heard there was an opening at the Museum at UCLA. So I decided to go home and interview for that because it didn't seem as if I was going to find anything in Europe. The day after I arrived, I went for an interview and they hired me. The position was for a half-time receptionist, and half-time exhibition designer. I did that for six months.

"Then there was an opening for a grants writer. The person who'd done the job was leaving, so I went into the Director's office and told him that I wanted to take her place. I knew I could write well, and by that time I was getting pretty tired of answering telephones and typing letters. After a couple of conversations and cajoling on my part, they agreed I could try it for a few months. I gave up the receptionist part of the job and started working half-time on grants and half-time on exhibitions. Then I became very successful at it. We were getting a lot of grants, and the museum wanted more, so it began to usurp all my time. Finally they upgraded the job to an administrative job, more of a management job, and it became a fulltime position."

Anne Bomeisler
Grants Officer
Santa Barbara Museum of Art

"Well, it was mostly chance. I had finished two years of college and decided to get married. So I determined that I would drop out of school for awhile and work. And one of the part-time jobs I had had was selling shoes. The district manager of a company I was working for found out that I was thinking of dropping out of school and offered me a job in their management training program. I perceived this as a temporary job for one or two years, until I went back to school, but since it was, quote, 'some type of management job,' I decided to take it and ended up staying for eight years."

Eric Bourdon
Assistant Director
Department of Beaches and Harbors
City of Marina del Rey

"In my freshman year at college, I sat next to a woman at lunch — she was a junior — who was going into speech therapy. I said to myself, 'I think that would be a neat thing to be,' and so I decided to see what it would be like. I started taking a few classes and it met a lot of my needs: science needs, helping needs. I knew I didn't want to be a teacher in a classroom. This was a real specialty. I could work in a school, in a clinic, in a hospital, or in private practice. By my junior year, I was enrolled in the Speech Therapy program.

"There was a second factor, too. There was a kid on my block who went to a clinic at Queen's College. She had such a remarkable change in her speech pattern that I said to myself, 'That's amazing! These people really *do* something. That might be a good field to get into.' But I don't think I would have gone into it if I didn't sit next to that older student at lunch. It was a real fluke."

Susan Glickman
Training Coordinator
Daniel's Jewelers

"About my junior year at Rochester Polytechnic Institute, I looked at my grades and discovered that I had a C-minus average in Engineering. That made me think that a career in engineering may not be for me, at least the kinds of jobs that were open to 'C' engineering students, which were either sales or production jobs, neither of which sounded very good. In those days, if you were serious about engineering, you'd go on for a PhD in Engineering and do teaching and research — at least at the school I went to. Given that I was destined for minor league jobs in engineering, I started thinking about what else to do. A fair number of people had switched out of engineering because they were going to fail, and had gone into a business or management major. That didn't look good to me because then it would have extended my time as an undergraduate. So I decided to finish in engineering and managed to *just* do that.

"In the meantime, the guy who had been my fraternity big brother had graduated two years earlier, and had gone to Harvard Business School. I saw him when he came back to campus. He said, 'Apply to Harvard.'

"I said, 'With my grades?'

"He said, 'You never know.'

"I did and I got in. I think that probably someone in the admissions office mixed up my records with some-one else's. I held the record for the person with the lowest grade point average to graduate in four years from Rochester Polytechnic Institute and go on to grad-uate school — *anywhere*. Much to their shock that I went to Harvard; even more to their shock that I gradu-ated from Harvard. For years afterward, when anyone in Chemical Engineering would be in academic trouble, they would say, 'Don't worry about it! Apply to the Harvard Business School. We had this guy, Goldhar, years ago...we never figured out how he got in, but he did.'"

Joel Goldhar
Dean
Stuart School of Business Administration
Illinois Institute of Technology

"I started pursuing a career in teaching when I was in college. I did that on the advice of my junior advisor who told me that he didn't see that I did anything well. After looking at my grades, he told me I should either become a geologist — because I got an 'A' in geology, or do something connected to English, because that was another good subject for me.

"I had never really thought about it. I had never thought about a 'career'. I never could think that there was anything that one could prepare for, for the rest of one's life. It just seemed like a ridiculous concept. But I had taken a few English courses and there was this wonderful woman in the department, and I liked what she did for a living. I don't think I'll ever forget her. She was a millionairess who owned a tobacco ware-house and was very rich from tobacco farming. She and her husband invited me and some other students over to dinner and she said something about my going into college teaching. I had never said anything about going into teaching.

"As it turned out, the Vietnam War was heating up...it was the mid-Sixties...and so I decided at that point that teaching made a lot of sense because teach-ers were getting deferments. I also saw it as an oppor-tunity — pretty much through her eyes. I saw that she never really talked a lot about English, but she used it

20

as a departure point to talk about what she pleased. She was really rather brilliant and always made circles back to what we were supposed to talk about. She had a unique way of showing that all forms of literature had a real meaning for our lives, and that someone who could synthesize that in a classroom was really valuable. I thought I would like to do that. I ended up teaching for four years. I think I did a good job — certainly no worse than any of the other teachers in my school. I probably did better because I was so motivated."

Art Kradin
Director of New Product Development
Tratec/McGraw-Hill

As you can see from these interviews, all of the people are now engaged in different careers than they originally pursued. In some cases, they're utilizing the same skills, but they have changed work environments. In other cases, they're utilizing different skills in the same environment. In most cases, they have experienced different levels of career floundering before finding a career they really liked. So what does this mean to you? Is this a suggestion that, since the job search is a process, and since you'll probably change jobs and maybe even careers a number of different times in your life, that it doesn't matter what job you start out with? That you should take whatever is available?

Definitely not! These examples have been used for only one reason: to show you that the job search is a process. With that in mind, you can approach it in a more reasonable manner. You don't have to worry that the first career you choose is the one you'll be stuck with. On the other hand, the fact that most of the people interviewed about their first jobs learned by trial-and-error, didn't have a systematic approach, and now have good jobs they like, doesn't mean a hit-or-miss philosophy is the best approach. Many people who use a similar approach aren't happy at all in what they do. These successful role models were interviewed to make a point. So what's the point?

The point is that, while the job search is a process, and that while you will undergo some career floundering before you find a satisfying job, the job search can be approached logically and systematically. If you realize there are over 25,000 different kinds of jobs and literally thousands of different companies you could possibly work for, it's self-defeating to accept a position that satisfies *none* of your needs. However, you must *begin* by making some sense out of this complex market. You must begin to narrow your choices. In short, you must target a career. That is the subject of the next chapter.

Target Your Career

There are two questions you will need to ask yourself when targeting a career. They are: What do you want to do? And, where do you want to do it? You will want to know this information because *everyone* will ask you about it. Career counselors will ask you. Employers will ask you. Your friends and relatives will ask you, and so will anyone else you go to for help. It's as if they somehow think that the moment you graduate from college, you should automatically know what you want to do. The reality is that you probably won't know. As was already mentioned, career floundering is a common part of the job search process, and everyone goes through it at one time or another. Be that as it may, they usually forget about it once they've found careers they like. Why?

Because it's a somewhat painful process and, besides, once they've been working for a few years, they can't imagine that they were *ever* so non-directed and uninformed. So when you — the recent college graduate — approach them for employment or advice, they forget what it was like and respond the way everyone else responds, and ask you, "What do you want to do and where do you want to do it?" Worse yet, they expect an answer! After all, they don't have the time to help you figure out what you want to do. Isn't that what you were supposed to have learned in college? And so it's somewhat of a Catch-22. They can't help you unless you tell them what you want to do, and you can't tell them what you want to do until they help you discover what it is. So what's the solution?

The solution is that you've got to help them help you. That means you need to articulate what you want in terms they can understand; to compartmentalize yourself into a package they can handle. In other words, you do need to be able to tell them what you want to do; what kind of work you think you're interested in; and, where you want to do it (i.e., in what industry and organization). The more specific you can be, the better.

The best way to begin this whole process is by doing self-assessment. That means you need to find out who you are. You need to look inward to isolate those elements that are important to you in a job. You need to start thinking about what you like doing, what you're good at doing, what functions you wish to perform, and the skills and knowledge you want to use and develop further. This is an important step even if you've already defined the occupation you're interested in pursuing. This is because many occupations are flexible enough to include a whole range of activities. For example, engineering positions might include research, design, and production in different degrees. If what you really like is research, then you ought to know that so you can pick a position in which research is the most important element of the job. A sales job might entail phone sales or person-to-person contact. It could involve selling an expensive product line, meeting with high-level corporate clients and making complicated presentations, or it might involve selling a high volume of low-cost merchandise to consumers. You need to know something about yourself to determine where you'd be more comfortable.

For those of you who don't know what occupation you're interested in pursuing, this step is essential. It's an opportunity for you to begin thinking about what you like doing, what you're good at doing, and what functions you wish to perform so you can begin refining your options until they're more manageable. Although some people think it's easier to get a job if they say they'll "do anything", this is not the most productive approach.

There are essentially two ways of approaching the job search. One way is to find out what jobs are available and to apply for them. The other is to determine what you want to do and where you want to do it, and to pursue it. Most effective job searches combine elements of both, and in either case, your search will be more productive and more fruitful if you know something about yourself. After all, it's easier to convince someone to hire you if you know what you do best. A fact of life is that everyone doesn't do everything equally well. And most likely, your achievement history — be it in school or at work or during leisure time — will suggest that you have some skills and abilities that are more highly refined than others. It is your ability to articulate what these talents are that will make you more marketable to employers. It is your understanding of what these are that will make you successful in your job search.

While there are a number of resources specifically geared to helping you determine what your skills and abilities are (they are mentioned at the end of this chapter) you may wish to begin this process by doing some self-examination. What you're looking for are peak experiences. As you reflect upon your life up to now, think about those activities you've genuinely enjoyed. Consider all aspects of your life, including work, school, and social experiences. What were you doing when you felt on top of the world? Running a 10-K? Organizing a speaker's program? Designing a new filing system for the insurance office you worked for? Learning to speak French? Attending the NCAA Championships for your college basketball team?

If this task seems overwhelming, because you've got 20-plus years to evaluate, then begin by organizing your background into manageable categories, like: school, work, and social environments.

SCHOOL

Consider all education and training, classroom and informal learning experiences. What have you liked best about school? Did you enjoy the small seminars more than the large lecture courses? Was it the personal interaction with other students, the professor/student relationship, or the goal orientation of being accountable for preparing a certain amount of work on a weekly basis that appealed to you? What does this tell you about yourself?

How did you handle your school experience? Were you the kind of person who studied regularly for classes, or did you cram for all your exams at the last minute? Did you enjoy taking tests or did you prefer writing papers? Were grades important to you, or did you just want to graduate? Did you seek out professors whose reputation or experiences appealed to you, or did you take classes solely because your major required them? Did you attend lectures that were not required? What kinds of lectures were these? Were you excited by certain subjects? Could you lose yourself in the library for several hours, researching a particular topic?

Did you involve yourself in any extracurricular activities? Which ones did you choose? Why? Did you become a leader in any club? Were you a casual member of several organizations or did you immerse yourself in one or two clubs? Did you participate in any internships? What did you like best about your experiences? Was it important to see the relationship between your coursework and its application to the real world? Were you attracted by the particular organization, industry, or task that needed to be done?

What does all this tell you about yourself? Are certain patterns beginning to appear? Are particular areas of interest starting to emerge? Have you learned anything about yourself or about the choices you made in school that you should consider when deciding upon a work environment?

WORK

Look at *all* work experience — part-time, summer, volunteer, internships, as well as full-time jobs. Do you like a variety of tasks, or would you prefer doing one task? What machines or equipment can you operate? Are they related to a specific job? Are there tests or procedures you're familiar with? Do they fit into a pattern with any of your other skills? Often, a significant volunteer assignment may be more indicative of a career direction than paid experience. Work in a political campaign, for example, may develop experience in coordinating volunteers, writing press releases, organizing fund-raising events, or other skills that have direct job applicability.

Work on a part-time basis, either on weekends or during the summer, may also have more job relevance than is immediately recognizable. Even if you worked at jobs that seemingly utilized none of your skills, you can still learn about yourself from these experiences if you approach them creatively. Compare and contrast the jobs you've had. Think about the different work environments you've been in. Consider the diverse people with whom you've interacted.

Did you like working as a waiter more than you liked working as a clerk in the insurance company? Why was that? Was it the pace? Do you like a faster pace and constant activity more than you like quietude? Or was it the environment? Do you feel more comfortable in less formal surroundings? Think about the summer when you worked as a salesperson in a department store. Did you enjoy interacting with people in a sales capacity? How does that experience compare with being a waiter? Would you rather serve people or sell them? These are the kinds of questions you need to begin asking yourself.

SOCIAL

Evaluate your social environment. What do you do in your spare time? What hobbies are you passionately pursuing? Are you a sports enthusiast, a musician, a writer, or a film buff? Do you enjoy cooking elaborate meals for guests? Did you just redecorate your apartment on a shoestring budget with dazzling results? Are you a whiz at fixing your friends' motorcycles?

These activities you enjoy may have important career relevance. An interest in wine-tasting could lead to a career as a sales representative for a winery. A love of travel might lead to a career in the import-export business. A passion for entertaining might suggest a position in a public relations firm.

On the more personal side, look at your relationships with your family and friends. Do you have a lot of friends, or just a few close ones? Do you like being with groups of people, or would you rather be alone? Are you the one your sister turns to if she needs advice, or is it your older brother? Are you patient with your grandparents or do you get easily irritated with them? What kind of person are you? What type of social environment do you like best?

Once again, these are the questions you need to begin asking yourself in order to determine what skills and knowledge you have that you would like to use and develop further. It's a process you will repeat over and over again throughout your career, and your approach will become more sophisticated and more refined as you gain experience. What you should learn, however, from this initial exercise in self-assessment is how to identify and categorize your skills and interests so that they begin fitting into easily recognizable patterns.

The best way to begin is by capturing these experiences on paper. Look at the skills you were using during peak experiences. What types of people were involved? What equipment or materials did you use? In the service of what goal or ideal?

Although there are no magic numbers, you should probably come up with six to eight experiences. Write them out in great detail, as if you were explaining them to a young child. Very specific experiences are easier to analyze. Now, put them away for awhile. When you come back to them, examine them closely for patterns of skills, themes of interest. Probably an isolated skill is not important. What you want to uncover are the patterns.

Once you've completed this exercise, have other people look at what you've done. Ask them to write down the skills you were using, and the values which seem to predominate. Self-assessment is difficult to do, because you're never objective about your own background. There is a tendency to undervalue your experience. An ideal group is two or three others who are going through the process. Each member is then equally committed to working hard.

Since the process of examining your background may be somewhat new to you, let us give you a sample scenario. Say that you are a sociology major with significant coursework in psychology. Your part-time and summer work experience includes a head cook/camp counseling

(text continues on page 31)

28

SELF-ASSESSMENT SOURCES

Career Planning and Placement Center. The services of a college career center will vary, depending on the focus of the particular office. They will tend to be oriented toward career planning and development, or toward placement. Those that are planning-oriented will offer career counseling services to aid you in identifying your career goals. Those that are placement-oriented will focus on job-search activities — resume writing, interview skills building, and the coordination of an employer campus interview program. Students and alumni can generally use these services for free or for a minimal cost.

Career Counseling. Career counselors may be able to provide a variety of different functions for you throughout the job search. Initially, you will want help in determining who you are, and what you want to do. One way they can provide assistance is through individual counseling.

Some words of advice: counselors, like everyone else, have different strengths and weaknesses. They also have varying levels of ability and different backgrounds. So, if you don't hit it off with one counselor, or if you don't feel this counselor can help you, feel free to talk with someone else, assuming your college counseling staff is large enough to employ a staff of counselors.

You must also realize that helping you determine "who you are" is easier than helping you determine "what you want to be". The reason this is so is because there are literally thousands of jobs and thousands of organizations you might be interested in. Since most career centers are not generally industry-segmented or occupation-segmented, because they're segmented in a different way (toward specific degrees, for example), the counselors don't necessarily have a lot of industry knowledge. It will depend upon the individual counselor.

Vocational Testing. Another self-assesment tool is vocational testing. The most valuable test for college students, in general, are the vocational tests which compare your interests with successful people in various fields. The Strong-Campbell Interest Inventory is the most

(continued on next page)

helpful measure for determining your interests. A values clarification measure may help you prioritize your wants and needs.

Be careful not to depend on the results of any test, however, as the sole method of determining your career decisions. Testing is only one way of helping you determine your career path, and it's no surefire measure of success.

Career Planning Workshops/Seminars. Many career centers offer a variety of workshops and seminars to help you at every step of the way in the job-search process. Since most students and alumni need similar information, it's obviously more cost-effective to service them on a group basis. While the functions, content, and quality may vary, they generally deal with similar subject matter.

Private Counselors. You only have to look in the Yellow Pages to see there are many private counselors who will agree to talk with you, test you, tell you what you might want to do, and take your money. Be prepared for their fees. Many of them charge anywhere from $25 to $60 per hour, and it's amazing how quickly that can add up. Some of them are good; some aren't worth the money they charge. Once again, before you start paying someone a lot of money for their time, be sure to check them out. Ask them what they'll do for you. Ask them how many times you'll have to meet with them. Ask them for the names of some of their clients. Talk with these clients. Find out how much counseling they needed, and how valuable it was.

Continuing Education Classes. Another option is to take advantage of career development classes offered through a university or at a local community college. Talk with the people who will be teaching the courses. Find out what they plan to cover. Discuss your needs. See if they think they can help you. Get the names of a few people who have successfully completed the program. Remember, the job search is not terribly easy in isolation. The other students, as well as the instructor, can be the start of a job-search network for you.

position at a resort, a waitress job at a popular college pub, and a sales job in the cookware department of a large department store. Since you helped to work your way through college, the only other activity you've had time for is membership in the Sierra Club. You've coordinated several hikes, and you've written articles for their newsletter.

When you initially look at what you've done, you see no recognizable pattern. After all, the jobs didn't exactly reflect your skills and abilities. None of them were intellectually stimulating, and none of them suggest the type of job you want for a career. Why you majored in sociology is now a mystery to you. Maybe at one time or another you thought of getting into counseling, but the time has passed and you're stuck with that degree.

You look at your background over again, and begin thinking in terms of the categories discussed earlier: school, work, and social environments. You quickly realize that organizing your background into manageable categories is a much better method of approach. It's much less confusing and gives you a point of departure. So you turn to the first category: school.

You think about your schooling for quite some time. You know you liked small seminars better than large lecture classes because of the professor/student relationship. Positive reinforcement is important to you, and the smaller classroom setting allowed far more interaction. You realize that this will undoubtedly be important to you in a work environment, as well.

You're still not sure why you majored in sociology, but you do feel you have acquired some good skills. You know how to do basic *research*. You *write* well. And you can *organize* projects very efficiently. You guess that you must have developed some other skills, but you're still not sure what those are. You think that maybe you need some outside help in analyzing this any further, so you make an appointment to see a career counselor at the college career planning and placement center. In the meantime, you're ready to move on.

You turn to your work experience. Up to now, you have been dwelling on the somewhat "menial" nature of the work you've done. But when you sit down and think about it in more positive terms, you realize that you did learn a lot about work in previous jobs, and that you always did well in work environments. Your bosses liked you. You were usually given supervisory responsibilities. You always got along well with people — both other employees and customers.

When you discuss this further with your aunt, who is a human resources manager at a social agency, she suggests that all of your positions indicate you have *"people skills"*, interpersonal abilities. In addition, the sales clerk, head cook, and waitress positions evidence an ability to *think on your feet*, an *aptitude for dealing with resources* — cash, merchandise, and equipment — and an *attention to detail.*

Beyond the specific experiences you have mentioned, she also suggests that your demonstrated capacity for working part-time and attending school indicates some additional abilities. They show you are able to *organize* your time well, and you can *set priorities.* It also establishes that you've had *exposure to different organizational settings*, and *diverse groups of people.*

The more you think about what she's said, the more you agree. You *do* have excellent *interpersonal skills*, and your *ability to get along with all kinds of people* is something you've always taken for granted. You are *well-organized*, and it has helped you juggle school and work without apparent detriment to either activity.

You're now ready to explore your social environment. Although you haven't had much time to participate in a lot of school activities because of your work schedule, you have been rather active in the Sierra Club. Hiking is an activity you like, and you enjoy being with people who share your interests. On the other hand, you also like hiking because it allows you to be alone. You are the kind of person who enjoys working independently, as well as with other people. In terms of your personal life, you have a very few close friends, and you would rather spend your time with them than with large numbers of people. You also have a very warm relationship with your family, and it's one that you treasure.

Although you're actually quite surprised how much you've learned about yourself in this self-examination process, you still decide to keep the appointment you've made with the career counselor at your placement office. And that's a good decision.

It's obvious from the start that the counselor has a much broader perspective than you do. She is immediately able to discuss the positive aspects of your education. First of all, she tells you to stop apologizing for your liberal arts degree. It's an asset because it teaches you to think, to look at the big picture. Further, sociology is a discipline that gives you an understanding of how people behave in groups, and your minor, psychology, helps you understand what motivates people. This is the kind of knowledge managers need, and the counselor feels it's an important asset.

She feels the rest of your self-analysis is rather good. But she does suggest that you look more closely at the extracurricular activities you've engaged in. The skills you developed from coordinating hikes and writing articles are quite obvious, but she tells you to look deeper. She discusses the importance of transferability of skills, those skills developed in school which can be transferred to a work environment. For instance, if you can write articles about ecology, you can also probably write about banking. The skill is that of writing; the specifics of banking can be learned quickly by a bright college graduate.

This meeting has been most productive for you. Now that you know more about who you are, what your skills are, and what functions you wish to perform — researching, writing, analyzing, working with people, and organizing — you're feeling much better, although you're still a little worried because you're not sure how this relates to a specific job.

There is good news and there is bad news. The bad news is that it may not relate to a specific job. The good news is that this is alright. What we're really saying is it would be just terrific if you could take all the information you've learned about yourself, feed it into a computer, and learn what it is that you should "be". But that's just not the way things work. The process is not that simple. At best, what you have learned from all this self-assessment is a little bit more about yourself. The value of this kind of information is that you are now armed with knowledge about some of the skills you have and enjoy using. That is something you should keep in mind as you enter the job search. As you learn about different occupations, organizations, and companies, keep in mind what you've learned about yourself. Use this information to screen out different areas that meet none of your needs, and utilize none of the skills you most enjoy using. That's the primary value of self-assessment. It provides you with a certain insight that will enable you to selectively pursue areas of interest, and eliminate others.

With that in mind, it's time to move on. But before we do, we would like to emphasize one point that we cannot emphasize enough. This self-assessment phase that you've just completed is, in fact, *never* complete. Rather, it's an ongoing process you will experience over and over again throughout your working career. What you think you want now may change tomorrow, a year from tomorrow, or ten years from tomorrow. That's not a problem, it's part of the process. The values you have at age 21 are generally different from the ones you have at age 30. The skills and abilities you've identified now may change once you're in a working environment and begin utilizing those skills. Although this seems obvious and somewhat simplistic, it's still worth repeating because many people lose sight of it.

Now that you've made an initial stab at who you are and what you like doing, it's time to figure out how your needs will match the needs of the marketplace. In other words, how do your skills and abilities translate into an occupation? How do your interests relate to the work of a particular industry? How will the needs you've identified match a company's needs?

In order to find that out, you'll need to do some labor market research. The areas you'll be researching are occupations, industries, and companies. Your objective will be to figure out what you want to do, and where you want to do it.

When people ask, "What do you want to do?", what they mean is, "What occupation are you interested in pursuing?" Do you want to be a salesperson? A management trainee? A planning specialist? Or are you interested in a career in marketing, writing, or computer programming?

When they say, "Where do you want to do it?", what they mean is, "What industry or organization do you want to work for?" Do you want to work in education or advertising or electronics? Are you interested in working for a large company or a small one? Would you feel more comfortable in a high-growth entrepreneurial environment, or in a more stable and secure workplace?

Since there are literally thousands of occupations, industries, and organizations you might pursue, it is extremely helpful if you can begin paring down the list. With that in mind, there are two ways to proceed. There is library research, and there is field research.

3

Do Your Homework

Chances are you will utilize library research at various times in your job search. A good time to begin is when you're targeting a career, although you'll undoubtedly return at many different stages. Each time, you will be looking for different types of information, and a general understanding of the library's career-related resources is important before you start.

As you are well aware, there are various types of libraries you can utilize. The best bet for any college graduate is the library at the career planning center of your alma mater. The larger libraries usually offer multiple resources. They have copies of numerous books on the job search. They have booklets on occupational information, prepared by the staff. Some have audiotape interviews where alumni and members of the community who have interesting jobs talk about what they do. Others have videotape collections in which they have recorded Career Day seminars or panels on different occupations or industries. Some have computer programmed instruction; others have microfiche information on careers. The best libraries will also have annual reports, 10-K reports, and company brochures.

If you're not living near the university from which you graduated, see if you can use the resources of a local university or community college. Many times, their career libraries are available for the asking. Another possibility is your public library or the business school library of a local university. It's a good idea to check out all your options so that you can utilize the best available resources.

Once you've found a good library, the research process is not that different than research you've done for college courses. What makes it easier is that there are essentially only three topics you will need to research: occupations, industries, and companies. What makes it more difficult is that, surprisingly enough, the kind of information you will want is not readily available in a few standard resource books. If you're interested in a career in business, there are directories that list corporations. If the field of arts and communications is what you want, there are specialized publications for that. In short, wherever your interests lie, you will have to familiarize yourself with the publications that specifically relate to that area.

OCCUPATIONAL RESEARCH

For those of you who are not sure *what* you want to do, you should start with occupational research. You will need to learn about jobs. You will want to search out information about job descriptions, employment figures, education and training requirements, earnings, and job outlook. You might want to begin by looking at the following resources:

● *Occupational Outlook Handbook,* published by the U.S. Department of Labor, Bureau of Labor Statistics. This publication provides information on about 250 occupations. The occupations are grouped into twenty clusters of related jobs. The information on each job includes a job description, employment figures, education and training requirements, earnings, and job outlook.

● *Occupational Outlook for College Graduates,* also published by the U.S. Department of Labor, Bureau of Labor Statistics. This handbook is organized slightly differently. Jobs are not categorized in clusters of related jobs; they are listed alphabetically. There are about 120 occupations included. In the introduction, it states that these occupations are those of greatest interest to college students and graduates, and are those for which a college degree is preferred or desired. The information in each occupation includes a job description, employment figures, education and training requirements, earnings, and job outlook. In addition, there is a section on *Related Occupations* in which they list jobs that may require similar aptitudes, interests, education, and training to the occupation you're interested in. There is also a section entitled *Sources of Additional Information* which lists the professional associations related to each occupational field. Associations are a valuable source of additional career information.

● *The American Almanac of Jobs and Salaries,* by John W. Wright, published by Avon Books in 1982, is another excellent resource book on occupations. Whether you're interested in a specialized field like sales, public relations, or teaching, or in a particular industry like finance, the airlines, or the computer industry, you will find job descriptions and an evaluation of growth potential as well as a full range of salaries for most levels and positions.

INDUSTRY RESEARCH

For those of you who are not sure *where* you want to work, there are two elements you should consider. The first element is: what industry do you want to work in? Although this is a very broad classification, if you can focus on an industry, it will make the research that much easier. And some of you already have a good idea of what industry interests you. You know you have always been interested in the aerospace industry, or the finance industry, or the agriculture industry, or the retail industry, and that is an advantage.

If you don't know which industry interests you and you need to learn more about different industries before you can make a decision, it must be admitted that this kind of information is not easy to find in general books on the subject. There are a few publications recommended, although with reservations. They are:

● *The U.S. Industrial Outlook,* which is published by the U.S. Department of Commerce, and which discusses 200 industries. The information here may be too technical. It includes industry profiles, trends and projection tables, trade data, sources and references, and employment information. If it is too technical, just skim through it to see if any industries look interesting to you. You can research them elsewhere.

Another somewhat common reference book is *Standard & Poor's Industry Surveys,* published by Standard and Poor's Corporation. Once again, it may be too technical in nature, but it does provide a great deal of industry information, including an analysis of trends and problems, background information, an examination of the prospects for that particular industry, and similar information. Whatever you can get out of it is worthwhile.

For the most part, however, industry information is easiest to get from professional associations like those listed under the *Sources of Additional Information* section of the *Occupational Outlook for College Graduates.* Another resource for finding out about professional associations is *The Gale Research Company Encyclopedia of American Associations,* which has a comprehensive list. If you contact those associations, they should be able to send you some general industry information, or at least be able to recommend books or trade publications on the subject.

For those of you who are not familiar with the term "trade publication", it refers to those magazines, newspapers, and journals that are devoted to information about a specific field or industry. Another source in which to find out about trade publications is *Standard Rate and Data,* a directory that lists all the trade magazines, newspapers, and journals in each industry.

COMPANY RESEARCH

The second element that you need to consider in determining where you want to work is: what kind of company or organization do you want to work for? You should begin making a list of companies that interest you as you start researching them. Initially, you might want to ask the following types of questions: What does the company do? What is their history? What is their reputation? What do they own? What are their sales and profit figures? Where are they going? What are their products?

There is only one general source we know of that discusses different companies in different industries, and answers all these questions. It is called *Everybody's Business: An Almanac, The Irreverent Guide to Corporate America,* edited by Milton Moskowitz, Michael Katz, and Robert Levering, originally published by Harper & Row in 1980. This book answers all these questions and more, and it is entertainingly written and comprehensive. The book includes more than 300 large companies, and their criteria for deciding who to include was based on size, product/service identification, importance, and interest.

Of course, there are literally thousands of companies they couldn't include. So how do you find information on these companies? The best source is usually the company itself. Some librarians and career counselors will recommend that you look at the *Dun and Bradstreet Directory,* or in the previously mentioned *Standard & Poor's Industry Surveys,* both of which can be found in the reference section of most libraries. The information in these books is quite basic, however: an alphabetical listing of officers, products, standard industrial classification, sales range, and number of employees. Generally, this is *not* the kind of information you're seeking at this stage. What you're looking for is something that has more meat to it. You will want to find out what the company does, what types of people they employ, what their future plans are, what their business philosophy is, and related information. The best way to find this out is from the company's annual report.

If a company is a public company, which means it is owned by shareholders, it will generally publish an annual report because it is required by law to make its finances public. Some libraries and career centers stock annual reports, but it is not a common practice. However, it is easy to call a company and ask for one. No one cares *why* you want it. You may be a potential investor.

In any event, once you get your hands on one, you will find that the format for annual reports is somewhat standard. The first few pages usually include a letter from the company president informing the share-

(text continues on page 41)

LIBRARY RESEARCH

Purpose
- Provides in-depth, unbiased information.
- Enlarges your pool of possibilities by identifying jobs, organizations, and industries of which you may not be aware.
- Locates names and position titles of key personnel.

What do I want to do? Occupational Research
- Job descriptions?
- Employment figures?
- Education and training requirements?
- Earnings?
- Job outlook?

Where do I want to do it? Industry Research
- Size?
- Stability?
- Growth potential?
- Salary averages?
- Atmosphere?

Where do I want to do it? Company Research
- Products or services?
- Reputation?
- Divisions?
- Growth record?
- Size?

Results
- Develop a list of job functions and organizations you wish to explore further.

holders of the company's progress over the last year. The next section is devoted to the company's activities, and the activities of their subsidiaries. The last section includes the financial information, and generally there is a listing of the company's executives and Board of Directors. The purpose of reading the annual report is to familiarize yourself with the company. The more experienced you become, the more you'll get out of reading annual reports. But initially, you should certainly be able to learn what direction a company is moving in; what new divisions have been formed; what the president's primary concerns for the new year are; and what kinds of people work for the company.

If a company is privately-owned, which means that it is not required to make its finances public, this kind of information is much more difficult to obtain. If the firm is a large, privately-owned company that is well-known, it might have been written about in a national trade journal, newspaper, or magazine, which would make it worthwhile to do some research on the firm. You might want to check the periodical indexes, notably the Funk and Scott Index, and the Wall Street Journal Index. If it is a small company, a listing in a local chamber of commerce or county business directory may be all you will be able to find about them, unless they, too, have been newsworthy. In this case, you can check the same periodical indexes listed above.

If a company is not incorporated and is run as a sole-proprietorship or a partnership (which would include many accounting firms, law firms, marketing research firms, consulting firms, and advertising agencies), an annual report is normally not available. In this case, you might find information from a trade association.

Another excellent source of information is the company newsletter. Many firms, hospitals, and community organizations publish newsletters. Some of these groups will send their house publications to outsiders who request them. To find out if a company publishes a house newsletter, consult the listing (arranged according to the publications' sponsors) in *Working Press of the Nation, Volume 5: Internal Publications Directory,* published annually by the National Research Bureau, Inc., in Burlington, Iowa.

As you look through all this research material, keep in mind your objectives at all times. What you're trying to target is what you want to do, and where you want to do it. So, as you begin researching occupations, industries, and companies, keep a list of the things that interest you. You should come up with some possibilities. In the meantime, don't forget the library's other resources. Look through the books on occupations that the library staff has compiled. Review audio- and videotapes that interest you. If they have a computer, use it; it certainly can't hurt. Look at any bulletin boards where jobs are posted. Are there any listings that interest you? Why are they interesting? Is it the job? The industry? The company?

Once you've completed some of this research, you have to isolate at least one occupation and/or industry of interest before you can proceed to the next step. If you're still not sure what you're interested in at this stage, take a stab at something — *anything* — because it is time to get out of the library and into the marketplace.

When you think of it, you probably do have *some* idea of what you might like doing. After all, you are not completely uninitiated. Look at your work experience. What have you learned about jobs and organizations? Maybe the only thing you've learned is what you *don't* want to do — ever again, if you can help it. Although negative, that information is helpful in narrowing down the occupations and industries to consider.

Now consider your parents, relatives, neighbors, and friends. Hasn't your father mentioned that the Eighties will bring about great changes in the banking industry? And doesn't your next-door neighbor work for a computer company that is attempting to expand into telecommunications? If these areas hold any interest for you, great. If not, pick something that does, or else you'll fall into the same trap that is a common problem among college graduates.

Some graduates like the library research phase so well, because it's so similar to the kind of research they did in college, they hesitate to leave the library. They keep on saying, "I need to know more. I'm still not sure what I want to do. There are a couple of industries and companies that look interesting, but..."

There are no "buts" about it. The skills identification and library research phases are only a part of the process. They're interesting, and they're fun to work at if you're research-oriented, but you can't dwell on them in hopes of staving off your entry into the marketplace. It's time to move on to field research.

4

Investigate First-Hand

Field research may be a new concept to you. It is actually quite simple. It is a research method in which you utilize people as a source of information. Up to now, all your research has been somewhat internalized. You've thought about who you are, and perhaps you've explored it further in a counseling situation. You've thought about occupations, industries, and companies that interest you, and hopefully, you've researched them. But now it's time to do a reality check.

The value of field research is that it enables you to test your assumptions in the marketplace. Sometimes, the research will validate your assumptions, and sometimes it won't. Often, an occupation may sound glamorous, prestigious, or exciting until you talk with people who are involved with it on a daily basis. Many times, the industry you've targeted seems growth-oriented, yet once you talk with a few industry leaders, you find that it is also glutted in the city in which you want to work. None of this may be obvious until you get out in the marketplace and start talking with people.

The other values of field research are more subtle. Field research provides you the opportunity to establish contacts in your area of interest. It allows you to familiarize yourself with the vocabulary of your chosen occupation. It broadens your exposure to the world of work by enabling you to investigate a variety of different jobs and working environments. And, it gives you interviewing experience in a non-stressful situation.

WHO TO CONTACT

Since you've already isolated an occupation or a potential industry of interest as a result of your library research, you're well on your way. The first step, then, is to begin talking with the people you know, to see if they know anyone who is doing the kind of job you want to do, or is working in the industry or for a company that you would like to work for. You can start out by talking with your family, friends, friends of friends, past employers, professors, and the counselors at the placement center, because they often keep files of alumni who are willing to talk with recent graduates. Don't be shy. Anyone you've ever met is a potential contact. If you're unwilling to ask favors of people you know, you'd better ask yourself if you really want a job. A reality of life is that people do favors for people they know. And it's far easier to get in to see someone if an introduction is made.

If you do have contacts, the only problem you might find at this stage is that these people are willing to help you, but they don't know anyone in the occupational field or the industry you're interested in. In this case, see if you can broaden your areas of interest so they can help you. For example, if what you really want to do is work in the personnel department of a hospital, and your contact knows someone in the personnel department of a retail department store, see them anyway. It can be a fruitful meeting because you can learn something more about the field of personnel management, and maybe *they* will know someone who works in the personnel department of a health care company.

In the same vein, if your contact has a friend whose business is not at all related to what you want to do, think about it creatively. For example, say the person is an accountant and you have absolutely no interest in accounting. Don't let that automatically dissuade you from meeting them. Accountants serve people in all kinds of businesses, and perhaps they can introduce you to someone you'd like to meet.

On the other side of the coin, your problem at this point may be that you have no contacts whatsoever. That's all right, too. It's quite possible to set up the interviews yourself.

SETTING UP INTERVIEWS

Once again, we're working from the premise that you've done your homework up to now. You've isolated an occupation or targeted an industry that you're interested in. You have also done some company research and have come up with at least six to ten organizations that interest you. If you haven't, reread the section on company research and do it. The next step, then, is to pick someone who works for that organization and write this person a letter.

How do you decide who to pick? By interest. If you think you want to be a recreational aide at a community organization, contact a recreational aide. If you think you want to sell computers, contact a computer salesperson. If you are an engineer and you want to check out what it's like to work at XYZ Company, contact an engineer who's working there.

How do you find out who these people are? In a number of different ways. If you've been conscientious up to now, once you have targeted an industry or a company of interest, you have been reading trade journals, company newsletters, local newspapers, and the like. These kinds of publications always list names of who's doing what, and where. The other way is to call the organization. If you're interested in sales, call the sales department. In most cases, the higher you call, the better. It's often easier to see a sales manager than it is to see a salesperson, and they're generally more willing to talk with you. When you call any executive on the phone, you will undoubtedly get his secretary. Tell her you need the executive's name and title. If she asks you why, and she probably won't, say you need to write him a letter. It's that easy.

The letter you write should be concise and to the point. The following letter is a good example, but don't copy it. The employers we talked with said it's always best to write your own letter. They can smell a form letter a mile away. In any event, your letter should look something like this:

2328 Westholme
Apartment 3
Los Angeles, CA 90024

April 30, 1984

John Smith
Sales Manager/Consumer Foods
Westside Foods Company
19327 Wilshire Blvd.
Los Angeles, CA 90036

Dear Mr. Smith:
I've read your annual report, and I find the Consumer Foods
Division to be of great interest. I'm excited by your growth
plans, and I'm impressed by your market position.

I graduated from UCLA -- cum laude -- last December, and I
am currently exploring career options. I've had part-time and
summer work experience in food-related companies, and I am
convinced that the food industry would be an exciting place to
work.

What I need now is information. I'd like to meet with you
to find out more about the food industry, and to explore the
kinds of opportunities available in a company like Westside
Foods. I have prepared a number of questions I would like to
ask you, and I will need 20 minutes of your time.

I will call you on Wednesday, May 2nd, to see if a meeting can
be arranged.

Sincerely,

Sam Cline

Sam Cline

This is a good letter because Sam Cline has done the following:

In the first paragraph, he lets Mr. Smith know he's done some research on Westside Foods. This already sets him apart from his fellow graduates who haven't bothered to do research. In the second paragraph, he tells Mr. Smith that he's an achiever — he graduated *cum laude* — that he has work experience in food-related companies, and that he's interested in Mr. Smith's industry. Whether you are actually committed to an industry at this stage or not, you should make the person believe that you are. Why else would they spend their time talking with you? But back to Sam Cline...now that he's aroused Mr. Smith's interest, he tells him in the third paragraph what he wants: information. He also explains that he's done his homework and that he will need only 20 minutes of Mr. Smith's time, which is a reasonable request. Finally, in the last paragraph, he says that he'll call for an appointment. And so he does. The meeting is set up for the following week.

PREPARATION

Preparation is one of the most important requisites for a successful interview for information. Part of the preparation should involve familiarizing yourself with the company and industry of the person you plan to visit. You've undoubtedly already done that when you were doing library research by skimming through their annual report or reading some general information on the industry.

The second part of the preparation process is developing some questions you need answers to. The questions will be different for everyone. They should be slanted toward what you need to know. If you need to learn more about an *occupation*, your questions will be oriented in that direction. You might want to ask the interviewee the following types of questions:

1. How did you decide on the career you've chosen?

2. What do you do on a daily basis?

3. What percentage of your time is spent doing what?

4. What are the jobs you've had that led to this one?

5. What are the skills that are most important for a position in this field?

6. What are the entry-level jobs in your area?

7. What kind of people do you hire to fill these jobs?

8. What are the advancement opportunities?

9. What is the salary range?

10. What types of training do companies give to people entering this field?

If you need more *industry* information, you might want to ask other types of questions, like:

1. What do you like about working in this industry?

2. What don't you like?

3. How is the economy affecting this industry?

4. What is the employment picture like in this industry?

5. Are there a lot of jobs in this industry?

6. What is the largest area for growth in the future?

7. What should a college graduate know about your industry before he or she applies for a job?

8. What are the professional associations your company belongs to?

9. Does your professional association sponsor any career day events?

10. What publications or periodicals should I be reading in order to acquaint myself with what is happening industry-wide?

If you need more *company* information, your questions will be different still. You might want to know:

1. Why did you decide to go to work for this company?

2. What do you like most about this company?

3. How does this company differ from its competitors?

4. What kinds of people work for your company? With what kinds of backgrounds?

5. What divisions do you have?

6. How many college graduates do you hire each year?

7. In which divisions are college graduates most likely to be hired?

8. What should college graduates know about your company before applying for a job?

9. Where can you get this information?

10. What advice would you give to someone who wants to break into your field?

Obviously, the questions you ask needn't be segmented the way these questions are. The reason the questions were presented in this way was to show how your orientation should differ as you explore occupations, industries, and companies. You will undoubtedly want to know a little about each area as you talk to different people. And your questions will also differ, depending upon how much information you can uncover during your research. If a company is a public company and has been widely written about, you shouldn't waste the interviewee's time asking questions you might have looked up. In this case, you might want to zero in on the more detailed or personally-oriented questions. If it is a smaller company, or you have been unable to find any information on them, then the sky's the limit.

The third part of the preparation is personal in nature. Make sure you're well-groomed and well-dressed. We discuss this subject further in the chapter on interviewing, but let us just say here that you should look *professional.* For men, this means a suit (or a sportsjacket with slacks) with a tie. For women, it means a suit or a business dress.

THE CONTENT

The typical interview for information consists of three segments: the ice-breaking period, the body of the interview, and the closing. The follow-up, which in effect is the fourth segment, occurs after the interview has been completed.

The ice-breaking period

Since you're the person who asked for this meeting, and since many employers are not familiar with the concept of interviewing for information, it's your responsibility to put them at ease. The best way to do this is to explain what the purpose of the meeting is at the start, even though you've already done it in your original letter. After the introductions, you might begin by saying, "Mr. Smith, I really appreciate your meeting with me today. As I mentioned in my letter, I'm interested in the food industry and I'd like to explore the opportunities available in a company like yours. So I've prepared a number of questions. Would you mind if I take notes?"

Mr. Smith won't mind because most people are flattered that you're interested enough in what they have to say to take notes. And now that you've explained yourself, you can move on.

The body

The body of the interview is where you ask the questions you've prepared. For a 20-minute meeting, you should usually prepare at least 10 questions. Some people give one-word answers; others are more verbose. You don't need to ask all the questions you've got, but you shouldn't run out of things to say, either.

A good policy for establishing a comfortable relationship with the person you're interviewing is to start out with questions that aren't threatening. For instance, a good way to begin is by saying, "How did you decide on the career you've chosen?" Or, "Can you tell me what someone in your position does on a daily basis?" A *bad* question is, "How can I break into this field?"

An important aside here: don't become so intent on asking all the questions you've brought with you that you fail to listen to what the interviewee is saying. Although there may be certain questions that you really want answers to, there should be room for spontaneous dialogue. There should be room to follow the interviewee's lead, and discuss related issues that you never thought of.

The closing

When you're interviewing for information, the closing is where you thank the interviewee for meeting with you, and ask for other contacts. If the meeting has gone well, the interviewee will probably be delighted to give them to you. It needn't be awkward if you handle it right. A good closing would be something like, "Mr. Smith, I can't tell you how much I appreciate your meeting with me today. I've learned a tremendous amount about what sales means in a company like Westside Foods, and it's a very interesting field to me. As I mentioned earlier, another area that I would like to explore further before making a final decision is marketing. Do you know anyone I might talk with in this area?"

Again, if the meeting has gone well, Mr. Smith will probably say yes. In that case, you should say, "May I use your name in setting up the appointment?" If you don't appear too pushy and aggressive, he'll probably say yes again. And now you've successfully begun the process of setting up a network of contacts.

The follow-up

This step follows the interview and is a very important part of the entire process. The follow-up is composed of two different elements: the evaluation, and the thank-you letter.

A thank-you letter is a really nice touch, and everyone likes to be thanked for their time. It can also serve another purpose. It's a way of keeping your contacts interested and involved in your search, so you can contact them again in the future and they won't feel put upon. The important thing to remember when writing a thank-you letter is to try to mention something that you learned in the interview, so the interviewer knows you paid attention. The following sample thank-you letter should provide a good model:

2328 Westholme
Apartment 3
Los Angeles, CA 90024

May 10, 1984

John Smith
Sales Manager/Consumer Foods
Westside Foods Company
19327 Wilshire Blvd.
Los Angeles, CA 90036

Dear Mr. Smith:

Thank you for meeting with me yesterday. Your enthusiasm was
infectious, and I must admit that a sales career in a company
like Westside Foods sounds exciting.

I was particularly interested to learn about the training
programs you offer. I am convinced that an opportunity to
participate in a program like the one you described could be
extremely beneficial.

I also appreciate your introducing me to Mr. Kelley in the
marketing division. I spoke with his secretary this afternoon,
and we've set up an appointment for next week. I'll let you
know how it turns out.

Once again, thank you.

Sincerely,

Sam Cline

Sam Cline

As was mentioned earlier, the second part of the follow-up is the evaluation. This is where you sit down and analyze the interview. You need to ask yourself the following types of questions:

1. Did you learn what you needed to know?

2. Do you have a better understanding of the occupation and/or industry of the person you interviewed
   than you had when you walked in?

3. Is this the kind of occupation or company you would
   like to pursue?

4. If yes, what did you like about it?

5. If no, what about it didn't you like?

6. What other questions do you need to know answers
   to before you can begin making some decisions?

7. What should your next step be? Should you interview somebody else who has the same occupation to
   get a different perspective?

8. Should you interview someone who has a different
   job within the same company or industry?

9. Should you return to the library and see what other
   options are available?

10. Should you make an appointment with a career
    counselor so you can discuss your findings with
    someone who is more objective than you are?

DECISION MAKING

After you resolve some of these questions, it will be easier to determine how you want to proceed. In some cases, you will find that the
occupation you initially targeted is the one you like best. For you, the information-gathering interviews will serve as validation. You now have a
much better understanding of what the occupation entails. You've
learned what kind of people they're recruiting for this field, and you plan

to market yourself accordingly. And you've made some excellent contacts.

In other cases, you'll find that your initial projections were way off base. The industry you thought you were interested in holds no appeal for you since you've met with executives from five different companies within that industry. Or the job you thought you wanted is not at all the way you imagined it would be.

So you come up with a new plan, and you begin the process all over again. If you've been working with a career counselor, you go back to this person and discuss what the problems are. Otherwise, you discuss the issues with friends or proceed on your own. The information-gathering phase for you has been illuminating. You've learned things about yourself that you hadn't known before. You've discovered information about the marketplace that is revealing. And although you're slightly depressed because you've seemingly expended a lot of energy in a direction you're not interested in pursuing, you realize that it is far better to learn all this now than it would be to learn it after you start working. So you've actually spared yourself a lot of aggravation down the road, and you're relieved about that.

The third possibility is that, as a result of all this information gathering, you're confused. There are a number of occupations and industries that look promising to you, but you're not sure you have the information you need to make a decision. In this case, a good way to proceed is to consider the variables that may affect your choice of a workplace.

Categories of workplaces

There are basically seven categories of workplaces: business, industry, education and welfare, arts and communications, health, government and public affairs, and science and research. You might start out by deciding which category interests you. Are you interested in working with goods and services, and the data and paper that accompanies it (which is what much of business is all about), or are you more concerned with products, which is the staple of industry? Maybe the glamour of the arts industry strikes your fancy, or perhaps a position in government will provide the security you require. Have you always wanted to teach, lead and motivate others, and are drawn to the field of education, or would you feel more fulfilled helping people solve their health care problems? If you're not sure, read on. The more information you have, the easier it will be to make a decision. As you begin isolating a category of workplace that interests you, you might consider a few factors relating to your choice of industry.

Growth potential

There are industries that are projected to grow rapidly in the next decade, while others will remain stable. For example, the electronics industry is rapidly expanding, while the steel industry is in a period of slow growth, or even retrenchment. The advantages of joining a rapidly expanding industry are obvious. There will be more jobs. There will probably be greater opportunity for advancement. On the down side, there may be less job security and more competition for the jobs that are available. So if stability and security are your top priorities, then you might consider a slow-growth industry. You can find out about economic trends by reading business journals, such as *Business Week, Fortune, Inc.,* and many others. There is also information of this nature in the *Occupational Outlook Handbook,* published by the U.S. Department of Labor.

Salary level

The salary levels of different industries are another important consideration, and salary levels vary considerably. If salary is a top priority, you should know that chemicals and electronics, for example, are high-paying industries, while social services and retailing are generally considered to be lower paying. This type of information should be readily available at your college placement center or your local library. It can be found in the College Placement Council's Salary Survey. Want-ads that describe similar and related jobs are another valuable source for salary data.

Atmosphere

Working atmosphere is another important consideration. Some industries and organizations are formal; others are not. For example, banks, insurance companies, and accounting firms tend to be conservative, while advertising agencies, media, educational institutions, and hospitals tend to be less formal.

Size of industry

The fourth variable you might want to consider is size. Does the industry you're interested in employ a lot of people, or are the numbers

(text continues on page 58)

FIELD RESEARCH

Purpose
- Tests career assumptions.
- Establishes contacts.
- Broadens marketplace exposure.
- Provides interviewing experience.

Procedure
- Isolate an occupation, organization, or company of interest.
- Set up an interview.
  - -Use contacts.
  - -Make cold calls.
  - -Send letters.
- Prepare for the meeting.
  - -Do required research.
  - -Develop pertinent questions.
- Direct the flow of the interview.
  - -Ice breaking.
  - -Body.
  - -Closing.
- Follow-up.

Results
- A targeted list of occupations, industries, or companies that interest you is created.

rather small? That might make a difference in your job-search efforts. For example, there are 100,000 people working in the television industry nationally, while 2.1 million people work in banking. Obviously, opportunities in banking are more plentiful.

Once you've begun narrowing down the industries that interest you, it is time to begin thinking about the type of company you want to work for. As you evaluate the companies you have already met with, you might want to consider the characteristics of an organization that are important to you.

Location

The location of a company should always be considered. The location of company headquarters and the location of its branch operations is important in terms of your access to company leaders, and your professional mobility. Most critical decisions are not made at branches, and consequently, most important executives are located at the headquarters facility. If upward mobility is a top priority for you, it's best to work at headquarters or be willing to move to headquarters further down the line.

So if a company is based in Cleveland, and if you will only work on the east or west coast, perhaps you should remove that company from your consideration. You should also be careful if you are considering industries that are specific to certain geographic locations. For example, publishing is primarily an East Coast career, while the film industry is centered in Los Angeles.

Size of company

If we can generalize, large organizations are frequently known to have good training programs, but they can also be quite rigid. Job functions are usually more clearly defined, and the hierarchy may be more firmly entrenched. Small organizations generally provide more diversity of functions, earlier responsibility, and more flexibility. However, they may not have the prestige of a large organization, and it is usually easier to move from a larger company to a smaller one than vice versa. Of course, there are exceptions to every generalization, but these are some of the variables you might want to be thinking about.

You might want to consider a few other variables, including *growth record.* Is the company doing well in its industry? Look at their annual report. Read industry-oriented information. Talk to their competitors.

Is their *product line* one that you feel good about? Does it have a quality image? Is that important to you? Are they considered an industry leader? Do you care? Do you like the *people* you've met who work there? Do they seem enthusiastic about what they do? Once you can begin answering these questions, you can turn to the occupation you've targeted and begin asking yourself different questions still.

Will the job you've targeted be *satisfying* to you? Do you know enough about what the job entails to figure out if it is the kind of work you like doing? Think back to the skills and values you identified earlier. If creating ideas is important to you, will you be doing that? If taking responsibility is important to you, will you be doing that? If experiencing variety is important to you, is that part of the job? Is the *salary* range acceptable to you? Is there *growth potential* in a position like this? Is there a *training program*?

These are the kinds of questions you should now consider because they will help you zero in on what you want to do. Up to now, it has been healthy to consider all your options, and to explore new options as you reject the old ones. It's beneficial to keep a flexible profile of what you think you want to do, and to change that profile as you learn new information about yourself and about the marketplace. And although this flexibility should continue throughout your career as you grow and evolve, it is now time to set some limits and make some decisions. It is important to stop considering everything you might like doing, and to focus in on what you can be satisfied doing *for now*. The stress is on "for now", because — as was mentioned earlier — there is a real possibility that your career plans will change in the future. But even if they do change, you've got to begin somewhere, and it's far easier to begin when your goals are well-defined. So before you proceed, you need to make some decisions right now: target an occupation or an industry that you wish to pursue. Once you've done that, you're ready to move on.

Beef Up Your Resume

M. PHILLIPS

1015 _____ alth Avenue   H___ dress:
Apart____   507 Nort___ Street
Bostor____ chusetts 021___   Houston, ____ 77024
Phone: ____ 7-1483   Phone: ____ 1-2341

education
1977-1981   BOSTON ____VERSITY   BOSTON, MA____HUSETTS

Candidate for the degree of Bachelor of Arts in June 1___,
majoring in Mathematics. Courses include Statistics and Computer Programming. Thesis topic: "New Application of Co-Linear
Coordinates." 3.4 grade point average. ____ the Elliot
Smith Scholarship in 1978.

Treasurer of The Mathematics Club. R____ le for $7,000.00
annual budget. Co-chairperson of Bo___ ___rsity's semi-
annual symposium on The Future of Mat___ ___ Assistant
Photography Editor of The Free Press. ___or and prize-
winner at local photography shows. H___ ___ establish university darkroom.

1973-____   HOUSTON PUBLIC HIGH SCHOOL   HOUSTON, TEXAS

Received High School Diploma in June 19___ Achieved Advance
Placement Standing in Calculus and Physics. Academic Honors all
terms. Assistant Editor of Year___.

expe____   DATA PUNCH ASSOCIATES, I___.   NEW YORK, N____W YORK

Mail Clerk and Courier for the Accounting Department. ____ ___n-
ized mail distribution and sorting system in the depa___
Delivered sensitive documents to the executive branch___

____mers   HARVEY'S BEEFBURGERS, INC.   HO____ ____EXAS
19__, 1979
               Began work as a dishwasher. Was promoted to short-or___ ___ook.

part-time   BOSTON UNIVERSITY   BOSTON, MA.____'SETTS

One of six students invited to tutor for The Department of
Mathematics. Also graded student papers and worked ___ a
Research Assistant in Theoretical Calculus.

part-time   BOSTON UNIVERSITY BOOKSTORE   ____OSTON, MASSACHUSETTS
1977-1978
               Floor and Stockroom Clerk. Resp____ ____es included arranging
               merchandise displays, customer s____ ___nd checking invoices
               against shipments.

personal   Enjoy photography, reading scie___ ____on, and playing bridge.
background   Published two articles in mathe___ ____ournals.

references   Personal references available u____ ____uest.

Let's face it. Once you've done all this research, it's time to face a grim reality of life: you've got to start looking for a job. Whether you're interested in a public relations job at a university, an engineering job in the aerospace industry, or a management trainee position at a bank, you can't pursue it until you have a resume in hand. And unfortunately, the thought of writing a resume is distasteful. You feel violated by having to summarize your entire life in one page. You suddenly wonder whether any of your qualifications relate to your chosen profession. You worry that your 3.2 grade point average won't compare with that of fellow graduates who managed higher GPA's. You feel anxious because your work experience consists of rather ordinary part-time, summer, and Christmas vacation jobs. And you feel frustrated because you have absolutely no idea of what employers expect from your resume.

Join the crowd. It may surprise you, but most people feel exactly the same way. If they graduated with a 3.2 GPA, they think it should have been a 3.4. If they majored in history, they now wish it had been business. If they worked at many different part-time jobs that were non-career related, they're convinced that their experience has no application for future employment. In short, they're convinced that *whatever* they've done, it isn't good enough. Why does this happen, and how do you deal with it?

The reason the resume writing process is so threatening is because most people know very little about the functions of a resume. They have no idea how employers use the resume or what they do with it. So when they sit down and try to figure out particulars, such as whether or not they should include a career objective, or what employers are looking for in the educational background section, they're at a loss. They can only project what employers might be interested in. And if you're a recent college graduate with limited work experience, you somehow sense that the value of your projections is questionable. After all, the only people who really *know* how they use resumes are employers, and they're not going to tell you their secrets. Or are they? When asked, personnel officials gave the following observations on the use and importance of resumes.

> *Q: What is the importance of the resume in the job search process?*

> "A resume as an introduction is of extreme value. It's a good initial screening tool to see whether you

want to interview a student...The initial contact with an organization is through the resume."

Camille Caiozzo
Director of Employment & University Relations
Getty Oil Company

"It gives us some criteria for screening out people. It allows us to distinguish between the run-of-the-mill graduate and the graduate who shows potential. It's very important. It's the vehicle used to introduce the student to our company."

Larry Colson
Vice-President/Industrial Relations
Litton Industries

"It's the most important tool in that I use it to screen out applicants and to create a pool of people I will interview. A resume reflects to me an individual's style, how they project themselves. On the objective side, it provides valuable information for my evaluation as to whether or not they meet the criteria for the job."

Jan Stein
Director of Personnel & Training
American Heart Association

"The basic importance of the resume and the cover letter is that it piques the interest of the employer. We have relatively few openings available, and in our advertising agency we get over one hundred unsolicited resumes a week...I dislike resumes that are cute. What I like is a basic straightforward, easy-to-read resume. It should be well laid out. You should have an understanding of advertising. You should know how to market yourself."

Beverly Seppey
Vice-President/Personnel Manager
Foote, Cone & Belding

"It's important. It's a means of introducing the person to us. If we're recruiting on campus, we can zero in on particular questions. In the office, it's a

screening and weeding device. It helps us decide
whether the person would fit in.''

John D. Hammett
College Recruitment Specialist
Bank of America

"It has two purposes. The first is screening. When
I'm screening, I want to see one piece of paper with the
bare essentials. I use the resume to see if they're in the
ballpark. If I'm interested in hiring them, I want to see
more detail — like a breakdown of their coursework.''

Britta L. Lindgren
Manager/MILSTAR Mission Control
Satellite Systems Division
The Aerospace Corporation

"If I'm going over it without the candidate, I find out
very little. However, with the resume and an interview,
I find out a great deal.''

Jim Heerwagen
Director of Training & Personnel
Carnation Company

"From our perspective, it gives the student the
opportunity to put his best foot forward in writing. In-
creasingly, that determines whether the individual will
get in for an interview...''

Delano D. Dinelly
Personnel Consultant
formerly Director of Recruiting
Coopers & Lybrand

"It helps us to remember the individual after the interview. Initially, if you get the resume at the campus
interview, it gives you an opportunity to look over the
resume and to slant your discussion to certain areas
you'd like to explore in more depth since you have such
a limited amount of time — twenty-five minutes at
most. Therefore, you don't have to hear the whole
story and waste twenty-three minutes of the time
regurgitating what's on the piece of paper. You don't

have to do that. Things like grade point average, major, other schools you went to, job experiences, and so forth are all there, and the interviewer doesn't have to go through each of them. The way I try to do it is I find something on the resume that I want to probe and find out more about. It also, for me, allows the interview to be more friendly, and allows me to take some of the nervousness out of the initial contact. Very often, I will find something in the resume that I can start the conversation with. 'Oh, I see you lived in so-and-so Massachusetts. Well I did, too.' And we can spend the first two or three minutes getting comfortable.''

Gene Ross
Director/Recruitment & Placement
Bullock's

As you can see, while employers may differ on specific points, they seem to agree on the basics. To generalize, all the employers interviewed believe the resume is very important. It *is* a screening device. It *is* your introduction to their company. It *is* your opportunity to put your best foot forward in writing. And in order to be able to do that, you've got to understand the basics of resume writing.

The purpose
Some people will tell you the purpose of the resume is to summarize your background. This is only partially accurate. The real purpose of your resume is to generate an interview, and summarizing your background is not enough. You've got to present your background in such a way that a potential employer will *want* to meet with you. You've got to stress your accomplishments. Look at the two resumes that follow. These women have exactly the same background, but they've presented it differently. Which one would you hire?

```
                          Martha Kelley
                     2507 Veteran Ave., #202
                     Westwood, CA  90024
                          213/472-3044


CAREER            A challenging position with a dynamic organization
OBJECTIVE         in the food industry utilizing the skills developed
                  through work experience and educational background.


EDUCATIONAL       University of California, Los Angeles
BACKGROUND        Cum Laude BA Sociology; have taken many additional
                  courses in Psychology
                  Active member of Sierra Club; coordinated several
9/78 to           hikes and wrote articles for newsletter
6/82              Dean's List, Alpha Phi Alpha, Sociology Honor Society


WORK              I. Bullock's
EXPERIENCE        1081 Weyburn Avenue
                  Westwood, CA  90024
                  213/208-0000
12/80 to          Job Title: Sales Clerk
present           Supervisor: Anne Kraft
                  Description: Sold merchandise in cookware department
                  Reason for Leaving: Still there
                  Salary: Beginning: $3.65/hr.; Ending: $4.49/hr.


                  II. Bratskeller Restaurant
                  1056 Kinross Avenue
                  Westwood, CA  90024
                  213/478-0000
10/78 to          Job Title: Waitress
9/79              Supervisor: Joe O'Brien
                  Description: Served drinks and food.  Occasionally
                  seated customers
                  Reason for Leaving: Conflict with school schedule
                  Salary: $5.00/hr. (average with tips)


                  III. Triple A Ranch
                  Route #9
                  Tustin, CA  92376
                  714/321-1234
6/77 to           Job Title: Head Cook
9/77              Supervisor: Jim Taylor
and               Description: Planning and preparation of all meals.
6/78 to           Supervision of dining room and kitchen personnel;
9/78              maintenance of kitchen, dining room, lounge, and
                  grounds.  Assisted in supervising small groups of
                  campers.
                  Reason for Leaving: Summer job; returned to school
                  Salary: 2nd Summer: $950 plus room and board
                          1st Summer: $800 plus room and board


PERSONAL          Date of Birth: August 18, 1959
DATA              Born and raised in Los Angeles; well-traveled
                  Fluent in Spanish
                  Interests and activities: Photography, film, music,
                  dining out


REFERENCES        Will be furnished on request
```

Cindy Martin
2751 Levering Avenue, #706
Westwood, California 90024
213/475-3320

CAREER
OBJECTIVE
An entry-level sales position in the food industry. The area of food service is of particular interest.

EDUCATIONAL
BACKGROUND
University of California, Los Angeles
B.A., cum laude, June 1982
Major: Sociology; Minor concentration: Psychology

Relevant coursework includes:
-Economy and Society
-Business Statistics
-Business Finance
-Elements of Marketing
-Advertising Principles and Policies

HONORS AND
ACTIVITIES
Dean's Honor List, 1980-82
Alpha Phi Alpha (Sociology Honor Society), 1981-82
Delta Delta Delta, 1979-82
-Membership Chairman, 1981-82
Sierra Club, 1980-82
-Hike Coordinator, 1981
-Newsletter Writer, 1981-82

WORK
EXPERIENCE
Salesclerk
Bullock's
Westwood, CA   12/80 to present

Sold merchandise in cookware department during the busiest periods, including nights and weekends, sales and holiday periods. Promoted items; received honors for being top sales-person during two consecutive holiday seasons.

Waitress
Bratskeller Restaurant
Westwood, CA   10/78 to 9/79

Served food and beverages in a fast-paced, popular college pub. Assumed hostess responsibilities.

Head Cook/Counselor
Triple A Ranch
Tustin, CA   Summers of 1977-78

Responsible for management of kitchen and dining facilities of a summer camp. Supervised staff of 10-12 food workers, planned and prepared daily menu for over 100 people, maintained facilities. Assisted in teaching cooking and baking to small groups of campers.

ADDITIONAL
INFORMATION
Have travelled throughout the U.S. and Mexico.
Fluent in Spanish.

Interests include black-and-white photography, foreign films, jazz, and undiscovered ethnic restaurants.

REFERENCES
Will be furnished on request.

The answer should be obvious. In general, Martha Kelley's resume looks like an employment application, not a resume. It's not interesting visually; in fact, it's cluttered. She has included too much information that's not of interest, and not enough about her accomplishments. We are left with no real idea of what she's able to do.

On the other hand, Cindy Martin's resume is much more appealing. It looks good visually. It's easy to read. And we can clearly see that Cindy is an achiever. She highlights her honors and activities. She's been successful at work. She lets us know that she's a top salesperson, that she's been in a supervisory position, and that she's got organizational skills. Who would you want to interview?

It is important to stress that there is no *single* right way to write a resume. There are many ways to present your educational and work background, keeping several ground rules in mind.

The resume should be tightly written, neatly arranged, and uncluttered; it should place your work and educational experiences in the best possible light, emphasizing your accomplishments and responsibilities; and it should clearly demonstrate your qualifications for the job you are seeking.

The three resumes which follow differ greatly in emphasis and design, yet each serves as a good general example of a resume that will be read instead of being placed in the "circular file".

JOHN M. COHEN
2412 Jefferson Boulevard
Madison, Wisconsin 53706
608/292-3362

CAREER
OBJECTIVE

A research position performing a broad range of
tasks, including survey design, data analysis,
and report writing.

EDUCATION

University of Wisconsin, Madison
B.A. in Economics, June 1983
GPA: 3.4 overall; 3.6 in major

Relevant coursework included: Macro- and Micro-
Economic Theory, Statistics, Social Science Research
Methods, Computer Programming. Additional course-
work in Sociology and Anthropology.

HONORS AND
ACTIVITIES

Dean's List; Economics Honor Society; Wisconsin State
Scholarship. THE BADGER Yearbook Staff; Intramural
Softball pitcher.

RESEARCH
EXPERIENCE

RESEARCH ASSISTANT
City of Madison Housing Department   9/82 to 6/83

Assisted in the design and implementation of a
housing need survey. Interviewed survey respondents.
Coded and analyzed data. Prepared final report and
presented results to city officials.

INVESTIGATOR
University of Wisconsin Business School 6/82 to 9/82

Assisted three finance faculty members in a variety
of research projects. Responsibilities included
model-building, computer applications.

ADDITIONAL
EXPERIENCE

MANAGER
The Reginald House   9/81 to 6/82

Managed the day-to-day operations of a student residence
including supervision of 12-14 assistants and administration of the operating budget.

Other part-time and summer employment included:
Parking lot attendant, busboy, theater usher, store
clerk, and house painter.

References and copies of research projects will be
provided on request.

PETER MANCINI
632 South Avis Avenue
Lexington, Kentucky   40508
606/238-8190

EDUCATIONAL   B.S., University of Kentucky, May 1984
BACKGROUND   Major: Electrical Engineering

                   Coursework included:
                   -Electrical and Electronic Circuits
                   -Passive Network Synthesis
                   -Electronic Signal Processing
                   -Pulse and Digital Methods
                   -Computer System Architecture
                   -Electromagnetics

ACTIVITIES   4-year Letterman in Varsity Soccer
                   Recipient of "Most Inspirational Player" Award, 1983
                   Co-captain, 1984

EXPERIENCE   SEASONAL LIFEGUARD for the City of Lexington;
                   promoted to DIVISION COMMANDER, responsible for payroll,
1981-84   scheduling and supervision of 15-20 guards at eight
                   different sites.

                   HEAD SWIMMING COACH, Kornell Swim Club; managed 80-100
1983-84   teenage athletes. Scheduled practices and meets, and
                   assisted in fund-raising events.

                   Additional part-time jobs as Bartender, Night Watchman,
                   and Nursery Salesman, providing 50% of support during
                   college.

INTERESTS   Auto restoring, waterskiing, backpacking, and photography.

                   References furnished on request.

MARION CHEN

1236 Salina Street
Santa Monica, California 90203
213/826-5512 (home)
213/928-3006 (messages)

GOAL   Public Relations

SKILLS   * Research and writing
                * Public Speaking
                * Fund Raising

EDUCATION   University of Southern California
                BA in Communication Studies, May 1984
                -received the Joan Mitchell-Williams and California State
                scholarships
                Senior Thesis: "An Analysis of the Home Video Market in
                Southern California"

EXPERIENCE   STAFF WRITER, USC Daily Trojan   9/82 to 5/84
                Covered news and feature stories, with emphasis on
                entertainment and the arts. Conducted and wrote
                in-depth interviews on subjects such as film actor
                Robert DeNiro and writer Saul Bellow.

                STUDENT COORDINATOR, USC Homecoming Weekend   Fall 1982
                Coordinated all facets of major university event attended
                by over 8000 students, alumni, and guests. Responsible
                for publicity, budgeting, staffing, and scheduling.

                ADMINISTRATIVE ASSISTANT, Smith, Smith and Kaplan,
                Attorneys-at-Law   6/81 to 9/82
                Assisted with legal research, office procedures, and
                clerical support.

ADDITIONAL   Fundraising Committee, Santa Monica Choral Association
ACTIVITIES   Pacific Coast Singing Society
                Currently singing with the LA Master Chorale; have performed
                with the LA Philharmonic Orchestra at the Music Center,
                Hollywood Bowl and on radio and television.

REFERENCES   Furnished on request.

The format

The most common resume formats are the chronological format, and the functional format. The functional resume focuses on skill categories. The chronological resume is structured by dates of employment. For the purposes of this book, the chronological resume is offered as an example, because it is the most widely used and accepted format.

CHRONOLOGICAL RESUME
(Sample)

NAME
School or temporary address   Home address
City, State, Zip Code   City, State, Zip Code
Telephone number (include area code)   Telephone number

OBJECTIVE   State clearly and concisely the level of job, function, and
                 type of company or industry you are seeking. Data should
                 reflect your present or short-range plans.

EDUCATION   Schools, degrees and/or certificates, dates.
                 Courses taken in/outside major related to employment objective.
                 Papers, research projects, etc., indicative of specific abili-
                 ties and knowledge.

HONORS AND   Honors, awards, and extra-curricular activities that reflect
ACTIVITIES   skills.

EXPERIENCE   Job titles.
SUMMARY   Names of employers, locations, dates worked.
                 Emphasis on:
                 -special skills or talents developed.
                 -experience gained that can apply to another job.
                 -personal characteristics that promoted success.
                 -unique contributions made or ideas initiated.

ADDITIONAL   Community activities. Professional activities. Hobbies and
INFORMATION   interests. Travel experiences. Language skills.

PERSONAL   Date of birth. Marital status. Citizenship/security clearances.

REFERENCES   State: "Will be furnished upon request."

The content

As you can see from the sample, there are only eight elements that compose most resumes. The first and last elements are easy to complete. The first is your name, address, and telephone number. The last refers to references, and the standard statement is always, "References will be furnished upon request." So we are left with six elements.

The first of these elements is the *CAREER OBJECTIVE.* A career objective is typically where you state the job, job function, company, or industry you're interested in. There are different opinions on the value of including a career objective in your resume, as is evident by the following comments of these employers.

Q: What is the value of a career objective?

"What's realistic in a career objective is for them to say, 'These are the areas I've studied. I've done well in such-and-such. I'm interested in such-and-such.' They should put down several objectives so that I can make a fit between what the company needs and what the student wants. What I'm interested in is: what do you want to do? What can you do?"

Britta L. Lindgren
Manager/MILSTAR Mission Control
Satellite Systems Division
The Aerospace Corporation

"I see objectives on a lot of resumes. If the objective is clearly retailing, and that's what you want, it's very interesting to find it there and it's good. But if it isn't definite and you're not going to stick with whatever your objective is, then don't put it down."

Gene Ross
Director/Recruitment & Placement
Bullock's

"It shows me that an individual has done homework about advertising. I don't have a prejudice if they don't know exactly what they want to do. They still should demonstrate that they know something about the differ-cnt arcas, but thcy don't nccd to havc madc a final decision."

Beverly Seppey
Vice-President/Personnel Manager
Foote, Cone & Belding

Including a career objective is optional, and you've got to make your own decision. On the positive side, since employers receive dozens of resumes daily, a clearly-stated objective allows them to save time by enabling them to quickly categorize your area of interest. An employer who receives a resume stating that a recent college graduate is interested in "an entry-level position in the sales department of a computer company" knows what position that graduate is looking for. On the negative side, if that computer company has already filled all their sales positions, but they *do* have a position in some other department, you may have specialized yourself out of a job. So what's the solution?

There is no solution. If you do decide to include it, your objective should reflect your short-term goals and convey your current employment interests. Be specific without limiting yourself. Stay away from cliches and meaningless phrases, such as "growth position", "dynamic company", or "responsible position". Try to include the following components: the level of the job you're interested in, the functions and abilities you want to utilize, and the type of industry or work environment that you want to work in.

The *level of job* refers to descriptions such as "an entry-level position", "a trainee position", or a similar description of the level of your expertise. A *function* refers to a *specific* area within an organization. Examples of functions include: research and development, marketing, personnel management, purchasing, and many others. A *skill* means an ability or area of expertise. Computing, counseling, designing, planning, and analyzing are skills. The type of industry or work environment should be self-explanatory. Do you want to work in the computer industry or the banking industry? Do you want to work in the health care field or in government?

Here are some examples of good career objectives:

```
OBJECTIVE        An entry-level position in marketing management in
                 the consumer products industry.

                              or

OBJECTIVE        Desire to participate in a management training program
                 in the banking industry leading to a career in the
                 loan division.

                              or

OBJECTIVE        An entry-level job in a newsroom, leading to writing,
                 reporting, or producing of broadcast news.

                              or

OBJECTIVE        A position in the health field using background and
                 experience in organizing groups, clarifying ideas and
                 problems, making public addresses, writing reports,
                 articles, and newsletters.
```

One last word of advice. The decision you make about including or excluding a career objective in your resume isn't irreversible. If you're not really sure what to do, type up two different resumes: one that includes a career objective, and one that doesn't. See what kind of response you get to each one. Another alternative is to exclude the career objective from your resume, and include it in your cover letter.

The next element you need to deal with is *EDUCATIONAL BACKGROUND.* If you have limited work experiences, your educational background represents your most marketable asset. The completion of a Bachelor's degree may be indicative of high potential. Most employers are interested in your total educational experience, which includes honors, awards, and extra-curricular activities, as well as the more traditional educational information.

Here are some suggestions from personnel officers about what they look for in educational backgrounds:

Q: What are the most important factors you look for in educational background?

"Obviously, the GPA is important, but it's not critical. We recognize that different universities have different criteria. A 3.6 from one school may be comparable to a 3.0 from another. Students with a higher GPA may have a higher probability of success. The differences above a 3.0 aren't critical. But if we're judging a 3.5 against a 2.0, it's important. Also, there is a preference for outside activities related to their major."

Larry Colson
Vice-President/Industrial Relations
Litton Industries

"It depends upon the position they're applying for. On the credit side, we look for accounting coursework and business courses. On the operations side, their major isn't as important. We look at interpersonal skills. What kind of people-related jobs or activities have the students been involved with?"

John D. Hammett
Recruitment Officer
Bank of America

"My personal opinion is that the emphasis should be on knowledge and skills rather than the degree; otherwise, we begin to exclude people who don't have degrees. But I would say that often a large corporation's position is that they want the degree and they want it from the best school. Why not get the best person with the best credentials if you can? The school makes an impression on the people that a company does business with. They also look for relatedness of degree. A published article is very impressive."

Camille Caiozzo
Director of Employment & University Relations
Getty Oil Company

When asked about education, many employers automatically discussed grade point average and course of study. This seems especially important in the technical areas, as one would expect. However, when the subject was approached in further depth with the generalists, it becomes evident that when some employers talk about GPA, what they are really thinking about is achievement. If your GPA is high, that's fine, but whether it is or not, think about your accomplishments.

In any event, the way to begin writing this section is to list the names of the colleges and universities you attended, in reverse chronological order; dates of completion or graduation; degrees/certificates achieved; major and minor fields; and GPA if it's impressive. Include special assignments, research projects, or significant information about related courses. In particular, you may choose to emphasize coursework unusual to your major that may be indicative of specific abilities and knowledge. For example, a psychology major with several courses in math, statistics, and computer programming who is interested in market research would obviously list these courses.

In the section entitled *HONORS AND ACTIVITIES*, which is often a continuation of the education section, you should include academic honors such as the Dean's List or honor societies; special awards of any kind; or scholarships and fellowships. List extracurricular activities, particularly those in which you maintained a position of leadership or where you were responsible for planning or organizing an event. If you weren't involved in any activities, or didn't achieve any honors, delete this section.

A few examples of well-written *EDUCATION* and *HONORS/ACTI-VITIES* elements follow.

SAMPLE ONE

EDUCATION   University of Michigan
B.A. in Anthropology, June 1981
Graduated Summa Cum Laude, GPA 3.9

Relevant coursework includes problem-solving techniques and applications, computer programming, calculus, statistics, research theories/techniques. Independent Research Project: A study of the urban migration in the U.S. of Eastern European farmers.

AWARDS/   Honors Program
HONORS   Phi Beta Kappa
Margaret Meade Award for academic excellence
Eastern Star Scholarship

```
                            SAMPLE TWO


EDUCATION        New York University
                 B.A., cum laude, June 1984
                 Major: Sociology;  Minor Concentration: Psychology

                 Relevant coursework includes:
                 -Research Methods and Statistics
                 -Introduction to Computing
                 -Group Process
                 -Industrial and Organizational Psychology
                 -The Interview: Scientific and Professional Issues


HONORS/          Dean's Honor List, 1982-84
ACTIVITIES       Alpha Phi Alpha (Sociology Honor Society), 1983-84
                 Freshman Honor Society, 1980-82
                 Sociology Club, 1982-84
                 -Membership Coordinator, 1984
                 -Newsletter Editor and Writer, 1982-84
```

```
                            SAMPLE THREE


EDUCATION        M.S. Degree Candidate, 1984; Major: Chemistry
                 California State University, Northridge

                 B.A. Degree, 1982; Major: Chemistry
                 University of California at Los Angeles

                 Activities:  Recreation Association, Vice-President
                              Sproul Hall, Floor Representative
                              Chemistry, Astrology, Math & Physics
                              Club (CAMP), Co-Chairman

                              Intercollegiate Volleyball, Team Member
                              Metro Camp for the Deaf, Counselor
                              Daily Bruin, Reporter
```

The *EXPERIENCE SUMMARY* is important because most previous work has some relevance to what you may be applying for, whether you consider those part-time or Christmas jobs "menial" or not. At least that's what the employers we talked with said.

Q: What is important to convey in the "Experience" section of the resume?

"I'm looking to see how they spent their time. If they spent their time on vacations, it's not important. If they utilized their time and worked, hopefully the work will be related to the position they're seeking."

Jim Heerwagen
Director of Training & Personnel
Carnation Company

"Relevant work experience is particularly important. Whether a person is used to working is also important. Being used to working helps significantly in the transition from campus to our work environment..."

Delano D. Dinelly
former Director of Recruiting
Coopers & Lybrand

"This is where action verbs are important. If they assumed additional responsibility in their job, they should mention it. They should stress accomplishments. Related experience is important, although experience doesn't have to be directly related, as long as there is evidence that their skills are transferable."

Ruben Garcia
Staff Manager/Human Resources
Pacific Telephone

Once again, what employers are looking for is achievement. They want to know job functions you had, and how well you did them. In other words, what did you accomplish? What unique contributions did you make? Were you promoted because of excellence? Did you come up with any new ideas that increased the efficiency of your working environment? Were you given supervisory responsibility? Did you gain certain skills that you can apply to another job? These are the kinds of questions that employers are interested in.

When you sit down to write this section, begin with your most recent experience and cover all time periods. Include a description of your responsibilities, tasks performed, and any special contributions you may have made to the job. This is where you discuss your accomplishments. Initially, think of your experience in broad terms to highlight skills gained, exposure to diverse people, and to various work environments. Consider which aspects of your work history are most important: association with a prestigious employer, a series of impressive job titles, or some highly marketable skills and abilities, and support this emphasis.

Since many recent college graduates have limited work experience, this section may include full- and part-time work experience, summer jobs, volunteer work, research study projects, graduate assistantships, military experience, and internships.

Some well-written examples of the *EXPERIENCE* element follow.

SAMPLE ONE

EXPERIENCE
SUMMARY

Manager
White Front Stores, Los Angeles and Sacramento

Directly responsible for sales, cash control, inventory, personnel, and customer relations in camera, jewelry, and liquor departments.

Hired as a SALESPERSON, promoted in three months to ASSISTANT MANAGER, and transferred to Sacramento. Helped raise sales and profit level to highest in Northern California.

Promoted to Los Angeles as a MANAGER. Registered constant increase in sales, held labor costs at lowest level in Southern California, received favorable reviews for sales increases, departmental efficiency, tight inventory and cash control, and excellent customer relations.

Salesperson
Jack's Camera, Beverly Hills, CA; French's Camera, Sherman Oaks, CA; Studio City Camera Exchange, Sherman Oaks, CA.

Part-time and summer employment to pay educational and living expenses. Ran photo finishing and repair departments, set up and managed mail order division, assisted in writing advertisements, sold and demonstrated all categories of photographic equipment.

SAMPLE TWO

EXPERIENCE   University of Wisconsin (1982 to present)
Department of Chemistry and Engineering
Madison, Wisconsin

Graduate Teaching Assistant: Teach two "Introduction to Organic
Chemistry" labs; tutor minority engineers in Chemistry.

U.S. Army Bioengineering Laboratory (1982)
Environmental Protection Research Division
Frederick, Maryland

Physical Science Technician: Participated in several research projects
that dealt with air quality control measurement. Devised
an efficient method of disposing of Hydrazine.

National Bureau of Standards (1979)
Washington, D.C.

Research Assistant: Participated in research in the area of Hetero-
geneous Catalysis, including determining the surface
area of catalysts and standardizing a procedure for
surface area determination.

SAMPLE THREE

EXPERIENCE   Administrative Assistant in a national political
campaign, 1980. Coordinated communications between
50 storefronts and the central headquarters in Atlanta.
Participated as a Staff Worker at the National Convention.
Received job offers from Chicago, Michigan, and Texas.

Counseling Intern at a local high school, 1979. Assisted
with the design of a feasibility study that could be used
in evaluating student participation in an employment program.

American volunteer on an Israeli kibbutz, 1978. Conducted
an in-depth study of a communal living environment; special
interests included child care and the status of women. Awarded
a letter of commendation for hard work and dedication.

The *ADDITIONAL INFORMATION* section is optional. It is frequently the place where people list hobbies, interests, and other activities. It allows you to show another side of yourself. An employer will often begin an interview by saying, "I see you are interested in tennis. So am I." This section may also serve the purpose of showing an employer who may be hiring you for a high stress position that you have interests which help you relax. Employers seem to differ on its inclusion, however.

Q: Should a person list hobbies, interests, and other activities?

"Why not? I really don't know how important it is. Everyone 'skis, jogs, and plays racquetball,' but it shows that they're interested in outside activities. I wouldn't waste a lot of time on this. Be brief."

Larry Colson
Vice-President/Industrial Relations
Litton Industries

"No, I don't pay attention to it. They could say that they're involved in community organizations or they might mention business affiliations. However, I really don't care if you play tennis or fish."

Camille Caiozzo
Director of Employment & University Relations
Getty Oil Company

"Yes, I think so. One of the things that's a problem nowadays is that we're limited in terms of questions we can ask an individual. I've been interviewing a long time. I'm interested in people or I wouldn't be in this line of work this long, I guess. I think that a person is not just a little slice of life you see in an interview, which is the way the government has pretty much got it stacked. I mean, you can't ask how many kids are in the family or what their mother or father do, and so forth, which in some respects added a dimension to an individual. Sometimes it can be a very interesting dimension. If they tell me that they are the only one in a family of ten kids to graduate from college, and that their parents come from rural Mexico, that's a fabulous achievement. I'd like to zero in on how that happened. Usually you find out that they had a fabulous mother and father, that kind of thing. Even if you put that you're interested in jogging or sailing or something like that, it's another dimension of your personality. It gives us something to talk about."

Gene Ross
Director/Recruitment & Placement
Bullock's

If you decide to include *ADDITIONAL INFORMATION*, be brief but interesting. If you do include hobbies, be as specific as you can. "Running 45-50 miles a week" is a more interesting accomplishment than "jogging", and "playing classical piano in a local performance group" is more interesting than "music". If you belong to any professional associations, speak any languages fluently, or have any unusual hobbies that are pertinent to your career objectives, this optional category allows you to mention it.

Some examples of interesting *ADDITIONAL INFORMATION* elements follow.

```
ADDITIONAL        Extensive knowledge of photography, widely traveled
INFORMATION       throughout Europe and North Africa, facility with
                  French.  Interests include pre-Columbian art, jazz,
                  and California wines.

                              or

ADDITIONAL        Tournament tennis player with national ranking. Mem-
INFORMATION       ber of a local bridge club with participation in
                  regional tournaments.  Gourmet cook.

                              or

ADDITIONAL        Evanston Hospital Association, 1981-1983
INFORMATION       -Volunteer Coordinator, 1983
                  -Co-chair of Annual Dinner, 1982
                  Member, Student Chapter of American Chemical Association.
                  Interests include running (10-K personal best: 32:38);
                  reading (modern American novels); playing the piano.
```

A *personal data* section is also optional, and is becoming less a standard part of the resume. You may include date of birth, marital status, citizenship, and security clearance if applicable. Do not include height, weight, color of hair or eyes, or health condition.

The *REFERENCE* section is the last element of the resume. As we stated at the beginning, it is customary to state: "References are available on request." Just be sure that you come to the interview with a typed list of good references. Good references are people who respect you, who are knowledgeable about your abilities and accomplishments, and equally important, who like you. It is well-advised to think carefully about who you want to use, and to ask their permission.

Beverly Seppey, of Foote, Cone & Belding, explained most clearly how references are used. "We always check references," she stated. "We want to find out as much as possible about the applicant. We ask about strengths and weaknesses. Character. Ability to get on with other people. Reliability. Punctuality. Attendance. How ambitious, how motivated, how connected the person is to doing well. We want to see a high level of responsibility, terrific performance no matter what the job is."

As you can see, even though professional recruiters may differ on the specifics, they seem to agree on the basics. The value of including their comments, however, is to let you know that different people will view your resume differently. There is no one right way to present your background; the rules are not etched in stone. The resume is like every other element of the job search process — you'll have to work on it, refine it, and maybe even change it as you go along and as your career objectives become more clear to you. After all, there are dozens of different ways you can present your background, depending upon the job you are seeking, and which skills you want to highlight. For example, if you're a history major who wants a career in computer sales, your resume should be different than that of a history major who wants a career as a researcher. That's because the sales manager who will be reading your resume will have different needs than the research department head who will be reading the resume of your fellow graduate.

This is not to say that the format of your resume should be different, just the substance. While one resume will highlight research, writing, and academic skills, the other will highlight leadership, achievement, and people skills. And yet, there will also be some similarities in the two resumes. Both employers will be looking for a well-written, well-

(text continues on page 86)

RESUME CRITIQUE

Checklist:

1. Is the text centered and balanced on the page?

2. Have you eliminated all errors: spelling, grammar, and typos?

3. Is there plenty of "white space" on each page; wide margins and space between paragraphs?

4. Could the resume tell the same story if it were shortened?

5. Does the resume avoid generalities and focus on specific information about education, experience, and personal information?

6. Have you avoided technical jargon unique to a limited field?

7. Do sentences start with an action verb?

8. Have you avoided the third-person and passive voice approach?

9. Is "I" used sparingly, if at all?

10. Do you cite specific examples of successful performance when it's possible?

11. Do examples quantify results?

12. Do all statements appear in proper syntax?

13. Are all statements parallel?

14. Have you avoided big words, lush adjectives, and superlative statements?

15. Have you used short, pithy sentences in brief paragraphs?

organized, and well-laid out document that is presented in a generally accepted resume format.

Now that you're familiar with the eight elements of the resume, you can see it's not that complex a procedure. However, that doesn't mean that writing a resume is easy. Writing a good resume takes time. But when you think of all the hours you spent in college, writing term papers that were not important to you, you'll realize that this is time well-spent. Since your resume is an integral part of the job search campaign, it may be one of the most important documents you'll ever write.

With that in mind, you should write it and *rewrite* it until you feel it's first-rate. Once you're satisfied with the content, look at the way it's laid out. Is it easy to read? Is the text centered and balanced on the page? Have you eliminated all spelling, grammar, and typographical errors? If you're satisfied that everything looks okay, then type it up and have someone else look at it. If the career counselor at school is someone whose opinion you respect, show it to him or her. If not, show it to a friend or contact who's got a good job, and see what they think about it. Or show it to a professor on campus. An outsider's opinion is very important. It will help you look at what you've done more objectively.

Typing it

When you get to the point where you have a final draft that you feel comfortable with, it's time to type it. If you're a good typist and you have access to a good typewriter with a clean ribbon, type it yourself. If you're a lousy typist, or if you don't have access to a good typewriter, hire a professional typist. Many typists advertise in college newspapers or local printing establishments, or are listed in the Yellow Pages. They charge an hourly or flat rate, and since your resume shouldn't be any longer than one page, it's a relatively easy job.

Reproducing it

Because of the advent of some excellent photocopying equipment, resumes can now be copied as well as printed. The decision is usually a question of quantity, rather than quality. If you plan to reproduce 150 resumes, you may find that it's cheaper to have them printed on an offset press. If you only want 50 copies, it will probably be less expensive to have them photocopied. One word of caution, however, if you choose to photocopy: the key to success is finding a copy center that knows resumes and has the latest copiers. Resumes done on a poor machine are not acceptable, and the money you save won't be worth the price you pay.

Whether you choose copying or printing, the cost of reproducing a resume is dependent on two variables: the paper you pick, and the number of resumes you want printed. It is generally a good idea to pick the best quality of paper available, usually a 20-weight bond, in white or off-white. Colored paper is not a great idea, even though some people would say it makes your resume stand out. Your resume should stand out because of its quality, *not* its color.

Personalize Your Cover Letter

The good news is that once your resumes are all reproduced, you're ready to move on. Although writing the resume may have been a somewhat tedious process, its importance in the job-search game cannot be overstated. Examining your background in the microscopic detail necessary to prepare a good resume is critical to the job-search process. What it has forced you to do is to begin thinking of your background in terms of what you have accomplished. And that is exactly the kind of information you will need to know for the interview.

The bad news is that now that you have your resume in hand, you'll need more than your resume to apply for a job. After all, no matter how well a resume is written, it is still primarily an accounting of your background. And even though you may have done all the right things in writing your resume, like stressing your accomplishments and relating your skills and abilities to the kind of job you're interested in, you should *never* mail your resume without a cover letter. Why?

To understand why, you just have to place yourself on the receiving end. What if you were an employer who received hundreds of resumes weekly, many of which included cover letters, and some of which didn't? You'd probably feel that a resume without an accompanying letter was an impersonal, unexciting, and rather disinterested approach to the job search. You'd wonder how you were supposed to know what the job-seeker wanted if they hadn't taken the time to write you a letter and tell you. You'd wonder why you should bother reading their resume, when they hadn't bothered to demonstrate any real interest in you or your company. After all, sending out "blind resumes" (resumes without cover letters) suggests a mass-mailing with no particular attention paid to a product, company, or industry.

As you can see, the importance of sending cover letters with resumes cannot be underscored enough, and as the following interviews will show, employers feel equally strongly about the importance of cover letters.

Q: How important is a cover letter?

"My personal feeling is that it's very important. It gives them an edge. Most applicants don't prepare a cover letter. Sometimes we get a xeroxed copy of a cover letter with our name typed in. That's incredible.

Preparing an individualized cover letter shows the company that the student is interested in them."

Larry Colson
Vice-President/Industrial Relations
Litton Industries

"Very. Never send a resume without one. Make sure it's concise. Mention the source of referral. Mention your area of interest. Ask for consideration. Say, 'This is where my interests lie.' Let them know what you want to learn."

Camille Caiozzo
Director of Employment & University Relations
Getty Oil Company

"The cover letter is important, but not as important as the resume. If a candidate did not include a cover letter and had a good resume, I would not exclude them. The cover letter serves as an additional tool in evaluating the applicant by providing supplemental information along with a summary of their work experience. It further serves to substantiate their qualifications. It should be short; I like to get down to the facts in the resume without having to read through a lot of gobbleygook."

Jan Stein
Director of Personnel & Training
American Heart Association

"Very. Especially because — in any advertising agency — there are a lot more people who want to get in than there are openings. It can set you apart from the group. You can demonstrate that you've done your homework. I'm always impressed when they are able to comment on a special campaign that we've done."

Beverly Seppey
Vice-President/Personnel Manager
Foote, Cone & Belding

"If it's a cover letter that is specifically developed for me, it's an added plus. The standard cover letter,

'Dear Employer:' is a turn-off.''

Ruben Garcia
Staff Manager/Human Resources
Pacific Telephone

"Very. Just a cold resume in the mail is a turn-off; big companies get hundreds of them. I don't know how many we get a week. I know that I get tons of them. We go through them very quickly. We have to. And we skim the letters, so if you can put something in those letters that is more than, 'My resume is attached. I would appreciate an interview'', you may get greater attention. If you can put something personal about yourself — any reason rather than the standard reasons that you're interested in a retail career or our company — that will catch our eye and make you stand out from the mob. The cover letter is very important. It shouldn't be too long. Never two pages. Probably never more than three paragraphs, and succinct. It should say a lot in a few words about yourself.''

Gene Ross
Director/Recruitment & Placement
Bullock's

Since most of the employers interviewed share the same opinion about the importance of a cover letter, it is important to explain the fundamentals. But before beginning, a few definitions need clarifying because there are many different names that career counselors use for the basic job search letter. This book will describe two different types of job search letters: the only two that are particularly appropriate for recent college graduates.

The first and most common is the *cover letter*. This is the letter you send when you *know* a job is available. It is the letter that introduces and accompanies your resume. The second type of letter is the *direct contact sales letter*. This is the letter you send when you *don't* know whether a job is available. It may or may not accompany your resume. It will be discussed in the chapter dealing with direct contact campaigns (Chapter 8).

(text continues on page 94)

THE COVER LETTER

Purpose
- Provides an opportunity to tailor your background to fit the job you're applying for.
- Demonstrates that you've done your homework.
- Allows you to suggest the areas in which your skills fit an employer's needs.

Content
- In the first paragraph, you should grab an employer's attention by describing why you are interested in a job with their company. Show that you've done your homework.
- In the second paragraph, relate specific experiences or educational accomplishments that show you have qualifications for the job by giving examples and relating your background to their needs.
- In the closing paragraph, request an interview and explain how you plan to follow up.

Results
- An interview is generated.

The purpose

The purpose of the cover letter is to introduce your resume to an employer when you are applying for a job that you know is available. While the typical job-seeker can conduct his or her job search with one version of the resume, the cover letter provides you an opportunity to tailor your background to fit the job you're applying for. You can amplify the pertinent information from your resume, directly address the needs and interests of the employer, and suggest the areas in which your skills match the organization's needs.

The format and content

The standard format for a cover letter consists of three sections. The opening paragraph is where you state the purpose of the letter. Generally, mention the job you're seeking, who referred you, and how you became aware of the organization.

The middle paragraphs (or paragraph) are where you expand upon the purpose of the letter. Often it's where you relate your skills and background — which are detailed in the resume you've enclosed — to those skills that are requisite to the job you're seeking.

The closing paragraph is where you request an interview appointment. The most common way of doing this is to say, "I look forward to hearing from you to see if a meeting can be arranged." Although this seems like a passive approach (and it is), some employers will get annoyed if *you* pursue *them*. It is as if they feel that, once they have the paperwork on you, the game is all over. It's up to them to let you know if they are interested or if they are not. That's a depressing reality, but that is the way the game is usually played.

Again, there are exceptions to every generalization, and sometimes a more active approach can work for you. If you do want to take a more aggressive approach, and if it's a local firm, you might want to say you'll call them in a specified period of time (Thursday the 2nd; next week; tomorrow afternoon; and so on). If the company is out of state, you might suggest a time you will be in their area for an interview, and call them before you leave to confirm the appointment.

The following letters are sample cover letters. They are effective cover letters because, in each case, the graduate has accomplished the two objectives for writing a cover letter. They have directly addressed the needs of the employer. And they have suggested the areas in which

their abilities match the employer's needs, by amplifying pertinent
information from their resumes.

1891 Creighton Way
Waltham, MA 02154
April 4, 1984

Lawrence Simon
Director of Marketing
Robert Anderson & Associates
833 Common Avenue
Boston, MA 02107

Dear Mr. Simon:
I have had an interest in marketing in the computer industry since
I worked in retail electronic sales during college. Our telephone
conversation last Wednesday confirmed my interest in the Market Research
Analyst position currently available at Robert Anderson & Associates.
Your company is particularly attractive to me in view of your plan
to diversify into mini-computer technology and applications.

In June of this year, I will be graduating from Boston University,
where I am majoring in Economics. While at BU, I have taken several
courses in computer programming, and I am familiar with BASIC and
FORTRAN languages. Additionally, my experience as a Research
Assistant has sharpened my communication and presentation skills, both
oral and written. Also valuable are the many opportunities I have had
to work effectively with my superiors and co-workers.

I hope these are the kinds of skills and abilities you are looking
for in a Market Research Analyst, and I would like very much to meet
with you to discuss this opportunity further. I look forward to hearing
from you at your earliest convenience.

Cordially,

Brian Felzer
Brian Felzer

9066 Butternut Street
Apt. B
Albuquerque, NM 87131
April 14, 1984

Katherine Ortiz
Director of Development
KLMR-Channel 57
10659 Chula Vista Way
Albuquerque, NM 87115

Dear Mrs. Ortiz:
I read of the position of Assistant Director of Development with
great interest. I have always been a fan of public television,
and the opportunity of raising money for such a worthwhile organization is very exciting to me. I am a devoted viewer of such programs
as "Great Performances", the Jacques Cousteau "Odysseys", and "Live
at Lincoln Center", and I treasure the thought of being able to
bring this type of programming to our community.

I will be graduating from the University of New Mexico in June,
where I am currently majoring in Public Speaking and minoring in
English Literature. I feel confident that my speaking ability
will allow me to make the kind of presentations the job undoubtedly
requires, and that my writing skills will enable me to continue
the effective letter-writing campaign that you have so successfully
initiated. In addition, I hope my varied part-time and summer work
experience will demonstrate my ability to work well with people.

I hope these are the kinds of skills and abilities you are looking
for in an Assistant Director of Development, and I would like very
much to meet with you to discuss this further. I will call you on
May 1st to see if a meeting can be arranged.

Sincerely yours,

Sylvie Drell
Sylvie Drell

P.O. Box 7142
Grand Tetons National Park
Tetons Village, WY 83025

July 10, 1984

Henry Smathers
Principal
Hemingway Junior High School
Hailey, ID 83333

Dear Mr. Smathers:
    My aunt, Carol Hutchinson, wrote me that you are currently looking
for a person who can teach mathematics and physical education. I am
pleased to say that I may be just the person you are seeking.

    I graduated in June as a Mathematics major, with a minor in Psychology,
from the University of Denver. For the last two years, I worked as
a tutor in an after-school program where I taught everything from basic
arithmetic to elementary calculus. My summers for the past four years
have been spent teaching hiking and swimming at different National
Parks throughout the country. As you can see from the postmark on my
letter, this summer I am in Wyoming. I also have experience teaching
basketball, working as a coach in Denver for several junior high school
teams. My greatest achievement ever was that one of my teams, the Denver
Diggers, won the Nationals in 1981.

    Mr. Smathers, I am really interested in the position at your school.
I know I could do a good job, and I would love living in Hailey. I have
visited my aunt there a number of times, and it is a perfect environment
for my interests. Since I realize that time is of the essence -- I'm
informed that you need to hire someone by August 15th -- I want you to
know I am willing to fly to Idaho to meet with you at your earliest
convenience. I look forward to hearing from you soon.

                                    Sincerely,

                                    Jane Hartley
                                    Jane Hartley

As you can see, although the content and tone of the cover letters vary according to the job, the purpose is the same: to generate interviews. There are some other similarities as well. All of these letters are addressed to a carefully designated individual — preferably the one who is likely to make an employment decision — and not just a title such as "Director of Personnel". Each letter is original. It is better to write ten well-composed letters than to write 100 standard ones. Although the task may seem overwhelming at first, or perhaps just a great deal of work, it gets easier with practice. What you find is that the same letter can be adapted to the needs and interests of different organizations you are contacting. Once you get into the swing of writing these types of letters, certain phrases and ways of stating information will become second nature to you.

Each letter is businesslike in appearance. It should be typed on a nice, heavy paper stock, preferably the same stock that you're using for your resume. When you have your resume reproduced, you can buy extra paper and envelopes of the same type of paper. It's a nice touch. The typewriter ribbon should be in good condition. The typeface should be conventional; don't use a script typeface because it looks amateurish. The copy should be good clean copy; there is nothing less professional than receiving a cover letter with typographical errors and erasures. It looks bad, and even if you have to retype your letter a dozen times to make sure it's correct, it's worth the effort. If you're a hopeless typist, hire someone to type your letters.

One last word of advice: be sure to keep photocopies of all correspondence. These copies can serve two functions. First, you can refer to them when you call up a prospective employer to arrange for an appointment. They will help you briefly and succinctly restate the purpose of the call. Secondly, use them as a diary. Keep track of the date and time of your follow-up calls, the name of the person's secretary, and any other pertinent information. And now that you're aware of all this, it is time to move on.

Use Your Connections

"Okay," you say. "Now I've done what you suggested. A little intro-spection here and there, some information gathering to target a career or industry of interest, a few weeks spent writing and rewriting my resume which I now have in hand, and some additional time directed towards learning the fundamentals of writing a cover letter... *now* what do I do? I mean, how do I get a job?"

This is a reasonable question, and it is time to address it. How *do* most college graduates get jobs? Once again, it seems best to ask the experts. Placement counselors at colleges and universities throughout the United States were given a list of traditional job sources, and asked to comment on their effectiveness. What follows are their comments on the most commonly-known job sources.

Q: What is the effectiveness of college/university placement offices in locating job sources?

"A service that is convenient for the student/alumnus, and it should certainly be investigated. Different offices have different tools or services. Depending on the fields of interest, it can have concrete vacancies or, at least, information on leads. Career counseling should be utilized by the student in addition to on-campus interviewing."

Marvin J. Roth
Director/Career Planning & Placement
Lafayette College

"Probably one of the most under-utilized resources by many undergraduates or recent graduates. Later on, you might pay $500 for a resume service, or $3000 to $4000 for 'interview grooming' by professionals. You can get the same thing from your placement office for little or no cost."

Jeff Wood
Director/Career Center
Occidental College

"This is an excellent source of contact, particularly for students seeking their first career-related position.

Direct access to opportunity, plus assistance in questioning other opportunities is usually available."

Greg Snodgrass
Staff Counselor/Assistant Professor of Psychology
Southwest Texas State University

Q: How effective are private employment agencies in locating job sources?

"Private employment agencies seem to be helpful only where the new college graduate can articulate his or her career objective very specifically in terms of the type of entry-level professional position wanted, and the skills the individual brings to the job market. For this reason, we find that the graduates who need the most help because their skills are not specific or widely marketable receive the least satisfaction using private agencies."

Jane H. Cordisco
Director of Career Programs
Chatham College

"Very carefully select agencies that specialize in your career field. Seek recommendations from people who have used the agency. Be careful about signing an employment contract giving the agency the 'exclusive right' to job hunt for you. That does not mean you can't search on your own."

Nancy Sims
Assistant Director/Placement Center
Northwestern University

"The people who work for you are usually the people whom you pay. If you don't pay the agency (the company pays a fee when you are hired), don't expect customized service. They are going to try to fit you into what they are looking for. Again, like state agencies, certainly use them with the correct expectations. You get what you pay for usually. You'll have better luck with agencies that specialize in particular occupational areas."

Jeff Wood
Director/Career Center
Occidental College

Q: How effective are executive search firms in locating job sources?

"Executive search firms do not, in our experience, provide or seek to provide services which are applicable to the level of the position typically sought by new, inexperienced college graduates. However, this is not as consistently true in specialized disciplines where the demand for new graduates exceeds the supply."

Jane H. Cordisco
Director of Career Programs
Chatham College

"Unless the BA/BS is a nontraditional student with some experience, it's my awareness that a search firm rarely takes on an inexperienced client."

Nancy Sims
Assistant Director/Placement Center
Northwestern University

"Be careful of fee. Realize the 'counselors' only get paid if they *sell* you a job, whether or not it's right for you."

Marvin Slavid
Senior Placement Interviewer
University of California/Berkeley

Q: How effective are want-ads in locating job sources?

"The pits! My biggest gripe in this resource is with the 'blind ads'. It is very dehumanizing, especially when you're discouraged anyway, to write a letter to an unknown person at a box number with an unknown company."

Marvin J. Roth
Director/Career Planning & Placement
Lafayette College

"While want-ads do not tap the 'hidden job market', they are a resource that should be utilized. Even the staunchest advocates of alternative search methods note that jobs have been landed from want-ads. Also, they've probably become more legitimate or helpful in recent years because many companies list jobs there to meet affirmative action requirements. However, one still has to deal with fake or exaggerated ads, blind-ads that may represent positions that don't exist...The main point is not to rely on want-ads."

Greg Snodgrass
Staff Counselor/Assistant Professor of Psychology
Southwest Texas State University

"We encourage students to use want-ads as a part of a well-integrated job search. In addition, ads are a good indication of the demand in specific career areas in specific cities and regions."

Jane H. Cordisco
Director of Career Programs
Chatham College

Q: How effective are personal contacts in locating job sources?

"These contacts seem to be one of the most effective ways a person can job hunt or at least identify possible career sources. Talk to friends, relatives, their associates. Hope that that opens up a network of people who refer you on if they're not aware of a job."

Nancy Sims
Assistant Director/Placement Center
Northwestern University

"Probably the most helpful...most jobs are obtained in some way through personal contacts. Therefore, it is important to develop and exploit every personal resource possible."

Greg Snodgrass
Staff Counselor/Assistant Professor of Psychology
Southwest Texas State University

"Personal contacts are people who can trust you, know you, and can in many cases vouch for you. They tend to be willing to invest more time, energy, and risks with you. You are also more able to reciprocate some day. Use them for contacts and be sure to let them use you when called. Reciprocation is an unwritten contact rule."

Jeff Wood
Director/Career Center
Occidental College

The five job sources isolated here are the ones that most college graduates know about. To generalize, the college placement counselors interviewed here uniformly agree upon the effectiveness of the first and last sources: college placement offices, and personal contacts. They are not big on employment agencies, as a rule; they don't think that most executive search firms are geared for recent college graduates; and they do not feel you should rely on want-ads.

This is a realistic outlook. Depending upon traditional job sources for employment can be harmful because most job-seekers' expectations are so unrealistic. You are sure you will get a job by visiting the campus placement office each week. When you don't, because the success ratio is in fact slim, you blame yourself. You feel there must be something wrong with you, rather than questioning the process.

You may not realize that only one in five jobs is likely to be advertised anywhere; that employers often publicize openings only if the jobs are hard to fill or are undesirable in some way; and that many employers fill jobs with their friends, people recommended by their friends or colleagues, or with people who have contacted them directly.

Be that as it may, since a small percentage of people do find jobs using traditional sources, these sources have been included in this book. And in fact, there are a range of sources that most students are not familiar with, and that counselors agree can be quite productive. The more sources a job-seeker knows about and utilizes, the more effective their job search campaign will be. With that in mind, let's look at the list of traditional sources.

COLLEGE/UNIVERSITY JOB SOURCES
If you've got a bachelor's degree, and the authors of this book assume

you do, colleges and universities are a rich source of information, contacts, and opportunities. Most people — employers and job-hunters alike — feel very comfortable about dealing with educational institutions. Somehow, there is a feeling that you will not be taken advantage of. Not only should you consult with your alma mater regarding available resources, but you should also check with all of the educational institutions in the area. Most will provide you with some assistance, the least of which may be library resources.

Placement offices

Generally, the placement office is the best source of career information and job opportunities. When employers are seeking a college graduate to fill a position, they are most likely to list the openings with the college placement office. Thus, the good news is that the placement office is the best source for locating *advertised* job opportunities for college graduates. The bad news is that the majority of openings will be for engineers, accountants, or "administrative assistants" (read: secretaries), reflecting labor market demands.

Campus recruiting programs

Representatives of employing organizations from business and industry, government, and education visit campuses each year to interview seniors and graduate students for career opportunities available upon graduation. Almost every large company maintains a presence on campus to recruit new professional talent; almost every college and university offers this program for its graduates.

Campus recruiting is limited in its value to many students for various reasons. The organizations that recruit on campus tend almost exclusively to be very large. The nature of the program tends to reflect the labor market. Probably up to 90% of the employers who recruit at colleges are looking for technical talent: engineers, physicists, chemists, mathematicians, computer scientists, and accountants. The job opportunities that comprise the other 10% tend to fall into very general categories: management trainee for a bank, merchandising trainee for a department store, sales representative for a technical company. A unique, one-of-a-kind job is probably never filled through the campus recruiting program.

Many placement offices offer services, in addition to job listings. They provide assistance with resume writing and interview skills-building workshops. Some go beyond the basic services to provide career counseling workshops — skills identification, values clarification, career decision-making — and job search strategy workshops. They also frequently organize Career Days, Job Fairs, and site visits, which are all vital ways to communicate with a variety of employers.

Campus career centers may also house an occupational library, which should contain "how-to" books for resume writing and job search techniques, directories, and the recruiting brochures and literature from those companies that interview on campus. Many placement centers have put together very creative materials that will help you in your career choice or job search. Be careful and check to make sure their literature is up-to-date.

Alumni offices

At some colleges and universities, a marriage is taking place between the placement office and the alumni office. Each needs the resources of the other. Alumni ties are very strong. Frequently, a variety of programs related to career issues are conducted for members of the alumni association. Recent graduates may tap into the network of contacts maintained in the alumni office.

At Wellesley College, for instance, files of alumni interested in helping new graduates with their job searches are maintained. At the UCLA Graduate School of Management, computer printouts of alumni are maintained by last name, by geography, and by company name. It is easy to see that, if you are interested in a particular company, it would be far more effective to write a fellow alumnus as your initial contact.

For this reason, it's important to keep up ties with the school from which you graduated. You can do this by subscribing to the alumni newsletter. You may read about a former graduate appointed to a new post who can be influential in assisting you. You may also want to see if your college has a local alumni group. They frequently organize worthwhile events, and are an excellent source of potential contacts.

Continuing education programs

These courses tend to be an adjunct to the usual university offerings, and are designed to update people in the field. They are normally taught by practitioners rather than the theoreticians who teach in the regular program. Many have some sort of placement activities as part of the program. Others can be a good source of maintaining contacts in the field — with both the instructor and with fellow students.

Student clubs and organizations

Many are organized around a particular area: Marketing Club, Association of Mechanical Engineers, and so on. Some are organized around a specific issue: Society of Women Engineers, Latino Management Student Association, etc. Contact these groups to see what types of programs they operate. Often, there will be career fairs, industry forums, and similar presentations. Many of these organizations produce resume books which they distribute to employers. The benefits are obvious.

Faculty/Administrators

Faculty often consult in industry, and that isn't restricted to just business and engineering faculty. An English professor may be developing an effective writing program for a bank; a psychology professor may be conducting a study on the effect of piped-in music on employee productivity. Likewise, administrators in many disciplines have contacts with a variety of employers through professional associations. Make a point of visiting faculty during their office hours to begin to develop a professional relationship. Faculty can be a good source of contacts, and can be asked to write letters of recommendation.

EMPLOYMENT AGENCIES

Consider using both private and public agencies. There are basic differences between the two. However, both owe their allegiance to employers.

State government employment services

Operating under different names in different states, these offices offer a minimal amount of help in the job search. Their staffs, although frequently well-meaning, are often overworked, harried, and burned-out. The office resources in general are at the whim of governmental funding, which lately has been quite meager. These offices are probably best used for interim employment; i.e., if you need a job, *any* job, to survive while you look for a good job.

These offices do conduct very good research on current labor market conditions, including which industries are hiring, or which have received new contracts or grants. Contact the office manager to receive these bulletins.

Private employment agencies

These agencies generally find people for jobs, rather than jobs for people. They are in business to make money by filling job openings they have solicited from employers. Thus, they tend to reflect the labor market. They will be heavy on openings for engineers and secretaries, and they will try to fit you into the openings they have, regardless of your career interests. It can be a most demoralizing experience. A scenario might go like this:

Agency Counselor: "What are you looking for?"

Graduate: "I'm flexible, but I would like something in market-ing."

Agency Counselor: "Too bad you wasted four years majoring in English. You should have majored in Business."

Graduate: "But I did very well at school and gained a variety of valuable experiences."

Agency Counselor: "I understand. Perhaps this secretarial position may lead to something else in marketing later on."

Our advice to you is: be careful! Make sure the agency is licensed. Make sure you meet the person who will be working with you. Don't sign anything you don't understand. Check with *Access: Directory of Private Employment Agencies* for areas of focus. The more industry-specific, the more valuable they should be.

Executive search firms

Executive search firms and employment agencies are related as personnel organizations, and both fill employer vacancies. However, executive search organizations are rarely appropriate for recent college graduates. They usually work at high levels, filling slots for experienced executives.

PROFESSIONAL AND TRADE ASSOCIATIONS

These groups may be organized in a variety of ways. Some associations are organized around an academic discipline, such as the American Sociological Association, American Management Association, and so on. Professional associations are organized by field, such as the Association of Social Workers, Institute of Electrical and Electronic Engineers, The Personnel and Industrial Relations Association, and so on. Trade associations are organized by industry, such as the paper industry, the computer industry, or the automobile industry.

Nearly all have regular meetings — national or regional — at which career information is exchanged. It's a good place for personal contacts in your field, and for information about future growth and change. For a complete listing of associations, consult the *Encyclopedia of Associations* and *The Directory of Trade and Professional Associations of the United States.*

Some associations may require that members hold professional-level jobs when they join, but many also sponsor workshops, internships, and apprenticeships for those trying to break into the business.

TRADE JOURNALS, COMPANY NEWSLETTERS, AND HOUSE ORGANS

Consult the *Standard Rate and Data* (published by Standard Rate and Data Service), a directory that lists all the trade magazines, newspapers, and journals in each industry, to keep you up-to-date on your field's trends and events, and on the movers and shakers in that industry. Trade journals are devoted to information about a specific field or industry, or about professional fields. Company newsletters are in-house publications sent to employees and designed for a specific public. Read through the newsletters and journals to get an idea of new areas of growth, new plants or departments opening up, and new directions in the field. Some publications even include classified listings for jobs, although these are generally for experienced personnel.

Other resources that may be particularly helpful for recent grads include articles of interest written by a professional in the field. Contact them to indicate your similar professional commitment. Suggest a meeting. Articles about people can also be helpful. When you read about staff promotions, you should realize that people with new assignments within an organization tend to take on new staff members to assist them. Promotions can also indicate possible vacancies. A third area of interest is information regarding new contracts, research grants, and similar information. New sources of revenue may mean new jobs. Even if the grant or contract is technical in nature, support staff is sometimes added in the areas of contract administration, research, and personnel.

SPECIAL INTEREST GROUPS

Various organizations may fit this bill: social clubs, such as sororities and fraternities; and issue-oriented clubs, such as women's groups, veterans groups, political organizations, and minority groups. These organizations may be contacted by employers who are seeking certain categories of people or those with certain philosophical beliefs. Although public relations is a major function of these groups, they may be able to assist with contacts. Check with these organizations to find out how they let people know about job opportunities and whether or not they keep resumes on file.

WANT-ADS

The classified job listings provide an overview of what's happening in a local labor market. Consider, for instance, the Sunday edition of the *Los Angeles Times* want-ads section for April 1, 1984, which consisted of over 50 pages. There were 18 pages of engineering openings; six pages of nursing openings; six pages of secretary/clerk openings; and five pages of openings for computer programmers and analysts. Those ads alone accounted for half the total. What we can learn from this is what kinds of jobs are in demand, and what types of companies are hiring in particular job categories. What we can also learn is which kinds of jobs are difficult to fill because many of the listings will be in the category of hard-to-fill jobs. When you think that a full page ad in the Sunday edition of a major metropolitan newspaper may cost over $10,000, you realize that employers would only spend that kind of money if their need was great, or if they couldn't fill the job through regular channels.

In spite of this, it is still a good idea to use the want-ads as a source. A good idea, however, is to read the want-ads only on the days of its major publication, since nothing could be worse than facing each day with want-ads. For most daily newspapers, that will be the Sunday edition. For specialized newspapers, the major edition is generally a work day.

Realize, before you start, that there are different types of ads. *Open-*

ads list all information: company and location, contact name, title, description of job, and qualifications sought. These ads are generally legitimate. They are placed by employers and the response is directed to employers.

Blind-ads are similar to the open ads, with the exception that you can respond to a box number. Most often, these ads are legitimate. Employers list vacancies in this way so they don't have to respond to unwanted resumes. You will, of course, have no idea who the employer is unless they contact you. Follow-up is impossible.

Catcher ads are the ads to be wary of. They are listed by employment agencies, and are stated as such. The heading are what we call teasers, which means they are designed to capture your interest. A few typical examples are: "Television Broadcasting (4 openings)", or, "Internal Sales/Marketing Consultants to $25,000 Plus Bonus", or "Immediate Openings", just to mention a few. These ads are intended to create a pool of job applicants, and tend to be gimmicky in nature. A word to the wise! Agencies have been accused of listing openings that do not exist.

Situation Wanted ads are placed by the potential employee. This type of an approach may be useful if your qualifications are particularly unique, or if you want to attract the attention of an employer who may desire these unusual skills. These ads will be most valuable if placed in special interest publications, such as an architectural journal, a sociological review, company newsletters, or any type of professional journal, to name a few examples. However, it's certainly cheaper and probably more fruitful if you send a letter directly to an employer rather than taking this route.

PERSONAL CONTACTS

Of all job sources, *personal contacts* are recommended most highly by career counselors, because it is the most effective approach. As stated earlier in the book, people are more likely to do something for people they know. And personal contacts will pave the way for you into the inner circle of an organization. Employers are specialists in fields other than employment — in marketing, in production, in law, and in many other areas. They look toward trusted people they know to steer new talent in their direction. It is much safer, for instance, to hire the referral of a colleague in your field than to take your chances on a want-ad. So how do you get contacts?

(text continues on page 114)

TRADITIONAL JOB SOURCES

Colleges/Universities
- Placement Centers
- Campus Recruiting Programs
- Alumni Offices
- Faculty/Administrators
- Student Clubs and Organizations
- Continuing Education Programs

Employment Agencies
- Private Employment Agencies
- State Employment Development Department
- Executive Search Firms

Want-ads
- Open ads
- Blind ads
- Catcher ads
- Situation-wanted ads

Professional and Trade Associations
- Academic discipline
- Functional specialization
- Industry

Trade Journals, Company Newsletters, and House Organs

Special Interest Groups
- Social groups
- Women's groups
- Veteran's groups
- Political groups
- Minority groups
- Handicapped groups
......and others

(continued on next page)

Personal Contacts
- Friends
- Relatives
- Friends of friends
- Friends of relatives
- People you have worked with
- Acquaintances in professional or social organizations
- People you do business with
- Sports partners
- College and high school classmates
- Current and former faculty

......and others

Start with your family. Ask them to think of all the people they know who might be able to provide a job lead. Your mother's old roommate is the manager of a bank. Will that bank be needing any management trainees? Does your father's fraternity brother have any openings in his advertising agency? Does your brother's girlfriend know of any vacancies in the Post Office in which she works? Remember, everyone you've ever met is a potential contact. That includes relatives and friends, families of friends, neighbors, college classmates, alumni who majored in your field, faculty in your major, faculty outside your academic major, former employers, sports partners, or people who know you professionally, like your clergyman, doctor, dentist, or hair dresser.

Once you meet with these people, it's up to you to take advantage of the meetings. They're not automatically going to know how to help you unless you tell them what you want. In most cases, the more specific you can be about your career objectives, the better. It's obviously much easier for someone to know which of their contacts to give you if they know what kind of a job you're looking for. In other words, it would be much easier for someone to help you if you said you were interested in a job in computer sales than if you said you were interested in "business". Being "interested in business" is so broad an objective that it's almost as bad as having no objective. On the other hand, you should also make sure that your objective is not outside the realm of your contact. For example, if your contact has a management position in a bank, chances are that many of their contacts will be in the financial industry. In that case, if you want to use this contact, it would not make sense to specialize yourself out of their realm by saying, "I only want to work for an advertising agency." They may not know anyone in an advertising agency, and then your relationship is finished. So obviously, if you are interested in advertising but your contact is from the banking industry, it makes sense for you to say, "I am interested in working for the advertising department of a major financial institution."

As you review the traditional sources listed above, you might be interested in this comment from Julie C. Monson, the Director of Career Counseling and Placement at the University of Chicago: "I have been musing over your questionnaire, and find that I prefer to respond with one huge qualification. The effectiveness of any traditional job source depends more on the attitude of the job-seeker using the source than anything else."

The authors of this book agree. The job seekers who have been the

114

most successful are the ones who have had a positive mental attitude. They have experienced the same rejections as everyone else; they've suffered the same disappointments, but they've always bounced back and moved ahead. If their resume wasn't getting the response they wanted, they would write another resume. If their phone calls weren't being answered, they would keep on calling. If their contacts disappointed them, they would search out new contacts. In short, they persevered until they were successful.

8

Initiate Direct Contacts

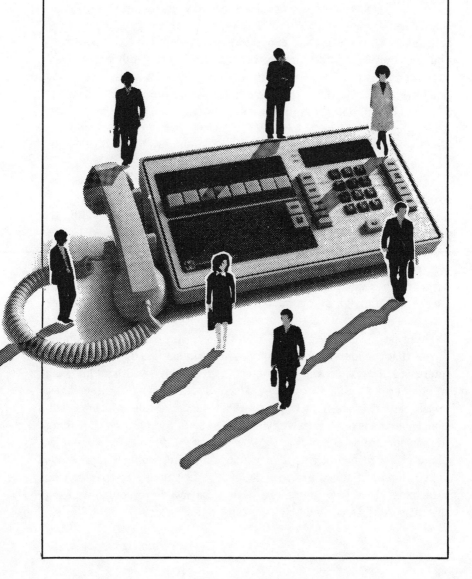

Let's say you've been utilizing traditional sources and making contact with a number of people. You've been active and you've been busy. You've been going to the placement center religiously, looking at their listings, and have even been on a few interviews from the leads you picked up there. You have also talked to a few of the professors in whose classes you excelled to see if they have any contacts. Two of them had only academic contacts, but the other one gave you a lead that you pursued. You have been to a few employment agencies because you saw ads listed in newspapers that interested you. Although your meetings at the agencies were not bad experiences, they were not too productive. The jobs they listed had already been filled, and the other jobs they suggested you apply for weren't the kinds of jobs you were interested in. You have also met with contacts you've developed through your friends, through alumni, and through a few social organizations you belong to. Although a few good leads have sprung up that you've pursued, nothing tangible has yet been offered, and it seems counterproductive to keep on waiting and hoping without exploring other options.

Actually, the option you'd like to explore most is the one you've uncovered while doing your research. What you learned there is that your first priority is a marketing position, and although you'd be willing to pursue it in any industry (in fact, you've already interviewed in the banking industry, the computer industry, and the cosmetics industry), your preference is the food industry. And although you're still willing to go on other interviews, what you'd really like to do is to develop a job search campaign that is industry segmented, because you feel there must be a more direct way to proceed.

There is. It is called the *Direct Contact Approach,* which simply means that you identify the companies in the industries in which you are interested in working, and you contact them directly — without knowing whether or not a specific opening exists. This is a simple, rather basic approach that is often successful. What's more, while utilizing traditional sources is often passive (you tend to be in the position of waiting for someone to do something for you whether it's returning your telephone call or responding to your resume), the direct contact approach is active. It puts all the initiation of action into the hands of the person who cares most about your job search — you! So how do you begin utilizing this approach? Once again, you start out in the library.

(text continues on page 120)

THE DIRECT CONTACT APPROACH

Purpose
- Enables you to apply for positions regardless of whether you know of an opening.
- Allows you to assume the initiative.
- Provides an opportunity to demonstrate your creativity and resourcefulness.

Process
- Identify companies that interest you.
- Determine key person who heads department in which you want to work.
- Research the company thoroughly.
- Write a direct contact sales letter.

Results
- Generate an interview.

LIBRARY RESEARCH

Before you start out, it's helpful if you are clear what your objectives are. Just because you've been in the library before, during other phases of the process, doesn't necessarily mean you can skip this step. Your objectives here are quite different, and you may be using some additional resource materials now that your search has become more directed.

Objectives

You have four objectives. Your first objective is to identify companies in which you are interested. Your second objective is to uncover the names and position titles of key personnel within these organizations. Your third objective is to learn some basic information about these companies, so you can approach them intelligently. Your fourth objective is to write them a letter. Let's begin with first things first.

Identifying companies

Your goal here is to compile a list of approximately 10 organizations you'd like to approach for employment. Some of you will have already completed this step in the information-gathering chapter when you did your company research. For those of you who haven't, rest assured that for whichever field you have chosen, there will be a directory that in some fashion describes many of the organizations in that field. One excellent resource is *The National Job Bank: A Comprehensive Guide to Major Employers in the Nation's Key Job Markets.* It is published by Bob Adams Inc., and can be found in many libraries and college placement offices. The book lists organizations, contact people, a brief description of an organization's principal business operations, and typical professional positions, as well as including an Industrial/Geographical cross-index.

Determining key personnel

Your second objective is to uncover the names and position titles of key personnel within the organization at which you'd be interested in interviewing. How do you decide who to contact? By interest. If you are interested in a position in sales, you might contact the Sales Manager. And if you are interested in an accounting position, you might contact the Director of Finance. If you are interested in a position in human resources, you might contact the Vice-President of Human Resources. The best reason for contacting people at these levels is because they are generally the decision-makers, and writing to senior officers has a few major advantages. First of all, they are usually on the lookout for talent. Secondly, they probably won't be intimidated if you're bright, enthusiastic, and aggressive — characteristics that can threaten lower-level managers who might view you as an antagonist. Thirdly, if you can enlist a key person in your job search, you dramatically increase your chances of getting an interview. Last of all, at the very least, they will send your letter to someone beneath them, which still works in your favor. There is nothing better than walking into an interview with a director whose boss has told him to interview you. It gives you a nice edge. So how do you identify vice-presidents, or other key management personnel?

Many times, their names and position titles will be listed in the directories, annual reports, or other resource materials you used when you targeted their company. If they are not listed, you can always call a company to find out. In any event, the person you contact should *never* be in personnel. The fact is, the personnel office is usually asked to recruit for a position only when it has become a reality; that is, after a job has been approved and a job description has been written. That's too late, and should be avoided. It doesn't give you the edge you want. What you want is to intervene in the process, if possible, before it gets to the personnel office, while it is still in the mind of the creator. It is that person's responsibility to know that so-and-so will be taking a leave in two months, that a new contract has been negotiated for the new fiscal year, or just that he wants to add a person to his staff. In other words, the person responsible for a particular function understands the scope of the staff needed. That is the person you want to know in the organization. That is the person who has the authority to make hiring decisions. That is the person to whom you will direct your letter.

One cautionary note. The anti-personnel orientation of this book is nothing personal. If you are referred to a personnel recruiter by someone higher up, fine. There are some excellent recruiters around, and they serve an important function in the employment process. But that function is generally misunderstood. In the hiring process, the function of the personnel office is to *screen,* not to *hire.*

Researching the company

The research process here is no different than it was in the library research chapter. You will need to read company brochures, look at their annual report, read professional and trade journals, check with professional associations, and perhaps even mount a field research campaign, in order to answer the following types of questions. What does the company do? What is their history? What is their reputation? What products do they produce? What are their sales and profit figures? Where are they going?

This time, however, your objective is different. In the past, you researched all this information in order to find out whether a particular company was the kind of company that could satisfy your needs. Now that you've established an interest in the company, your objective is to find out what the employer's needs are, and how you can help satisfy those needs.

Unless you have an inside contact, it will be difficult to ascertain an employer's *specific* needs because everybody's needs are different. Their needs are different, depending upon what they do. If an employer is a sales manager, her need may be to increase sales. If an employer is a television producer, her need may be 10 new story ideas for a series. And their needs might be different even if they have the same job, but work for different organizations. For example, one purchasing director's primary need may be increasing quality while a different purchasing director at another company might be more interested in reducing costs.

Obviously, this kind of specific information is very difficult to obtain. It is mentioned only to introduce you to the concept that *need satisfaction* is of primary importance in the job search game, and many people don't realize it. What they are concerned with is their own needs, wants, and satisfactions, and they don't even consider that employers must have a whole range of needs, wants, and satisfactions of their own. If you *do* understand this premise, you are way ahead of the game. If you can incorporate this premise into your job search, you will increase your odds for success enormously. Why? Because *need satisfaction* is a basic tenet of sales, and that is what the job search is all about. It's about selling yourself. It's about letting employers know you're interested in what they're interested in. It's about convincing them that you can help them satisfy *their* needs. With that in mind, let's look at how you can research a company to uncover those needs.

Since identifying *specific* needs is almost impossible unless you have an inside contact, it is important to explore the alternative, identifying *general* needs. This is far easier. If you've been doing your homework, chances are you've already identified some general needs. Let's go back to your field research.

As you began identifying an industry and companies of interest, you met with a number of people. You asked them occupation-oriented questions, industry-oriented questions, and company-oriented questions. What did you learn? If your field of interest was banking, you probably learned that the nature of banking is rapidly changing. Banks are becoming more marketing-oriented and are offering a full range of services they never offered before. If your field of interest was education or social services, you probably learned that as federal and state monies are cut, educational and social service organizations are enhancing their own fundraising efforts, and that raising money is now a top priority. And if your field of interest is the oil industry, what you should be aware of is that a priority of oil companies is exploring alternate energy sources in order to reduce their dependence on foreign oil.

Although these seem like simple realizations, and you probably learned far more than this, it is the accumulation of this kind of information that will prove to an employer that you understand the firm's general needs. All you have to do now is take it one step further. You need to think about how your skills, your background, and your interests relate to these needs. You need to convince an employer that your interests and concerns are the same as the firm's. That's not difficult if you think about it creatively, and once you've come up with a few good ideas, you're ready to sit down and write your letter.

The direct contact sales letter

You send a direct contact sales letter when you're interested in a particular company but do not know whether or not a specific opening exists at this time. The strategy is that a well-written letter directed to the right person may net a job opportunity whether the company is recruiting for that position or not.

Many counselors call this type of letter a *letter of inquiry*, but the authors of this book feel this is an inappropriate name. Sending a letter of inquiry suggests you're merely inquiring if a position exists, and that's a passive posture. Sending a *direct contact sales letter* suggests you arc going to *sell* somconc on hiring you, whcthcr thc company is looking for someone or not. The difference is clear.

Another important aspect of the direct contact sales letter is that it doesn't necessarily have to accompany your resume. It may stand alone. The pros and cons of including a resume are strategic in nature. If you want to work for a company, and your background is perfectly suited to that company — your skills, abilities, and potential will *wow* them — include your resume, by all means. On the other hand, if you want to work for a company, but your research leads you to believe you can sell them on hiring you *only* if you can get in the door, then don't include your resume. There's no advantage.

The format and content

The format for writing a direct contact sales letter is similar to that of a cover letter. It's the content that's different. The opening paragraph of a cover letter is where you state the purpose of the letter; it's where you mention the job you're seeking. In the direct contact sales letter, the opening paragraph is where you give employers a good reason for meeting with you. It is where you let them know you are aware of their needs, and that you've thought of some solutions, or that you're know-ledgeable about industry issues and that you're committed to working on them. The first paragraph is *never* where you mention you are seek-ing employment. Why?

There is one very good reason. It is because most key-level executives refer all job-seeking letters to underlings or to the personnel depart-ment. That's because they don't have time to interview every Tom, Dick, or Sally whose resume they receive. So you probably won't get in to see them if yours is just another cover letter. On the other hand, if your letter is more than that — if it piques their interest and suggests to them that you're someone different — you might very well get in to see them.

The middle paragraphs are where you expand on the purpose of the letter. Rather than just discussing your skills and background, as you would in a cover letter, this is the place for a "teaser", as they say in television news. The purpose of a "teaser" is to give your audience enough information to captivate their interest, but not enough to give the whole story away. You will want to give the employer enough infor-mation about your ideas so they want to meet with you, but you don't want to give them too many details before you get in the door because there's no reason for them to see you.

The last paragraph is where you request an interview appointment. And this time, you don't have to be at all passive like you were with the cover letter. Don't ever say, "I look forward to hearing from you to see if a meeting can be arranged." It's a different ballgame this time, and the game is just beginning. A much better approach is for you to assume control of your own fate, and specify how *you* plan to follow up. Therefore, you should always conclude with the more specific, "I will call you on Thursday, April 6th, to see if a meeting can be arranged." This approach leaves nothing to chance and suggests an underlying sense of self-confidence and professionalism.

The three letters that follow are all good examples of effective direct contact sales letters. As you can see, the people who wrote them did their research, gained familiarity with the company's products, and were able to suggest how their skills might meet the company's needs.

607 Oak Street
St. Paul, MN 55105
June 30, 1984

John Babton
Executive Vice-President
Consumer Foods
Natural Products Company
9200 Oak Street
Minneapolis, MN 55440

Dear Mr. Babton:
    In looking through your annual report, two items jumped out
at me. On the one hand, I was delighted to read that the Fashion
Division grew at a rate of 37.4 percent, and on the other hand,
I was dismayed to read that results from the company's frozen
food business were mixed, reflecting overall trends in their
market segment. Of course, this didn't surprise me, because at a
recent meeting at Westside Foods Company, I learned the frozen
food business is off, industry-wide.

    I have been thinking about this a lot, and I have a marketing
idea for increasing the sales of frozen food products that I
would like to discuss with you. You mention in your annual report
that your growth plans include "taking advantage of evolving life-
styles and the needs of increased numbers of women in the work-
force." Surely, these women are the target market segment who buy
frozen foods. What would you think about hosting cocktail parties
at key locations and serving your line of frozen food products to
this target market segment?

    I think it might be a really interesting idea, one that I would
like to discuss the possibility of working on for Natural Products.
I've done this on a trial basis at my college apartment in Los
Angeles, where I invited a number of soon-to-be-working women, and
it was a big success. Now that I've moved back to the Midwest, I
would like to discuss those results with you.

    Because it is difficult to reach me by telephone, I will call
you on July 7th to see if a meeting can be arranged.

Sincerely,

Chris Thompson
Chris Thompson

Obviously, this is a letter Mr. Babton won't be able to ignore. It's interesting. It's inventive. And it's creative. Chris Thompson has demonstrated he's a creative thinker, that he knows something about Mr. Babton's business and that it might be worthwhile for Mr. Babton to talk with him. That's the most you can ask from one of these letters. If this particular letter seems too complex for you, a few other examples follow.

233E Comstock Hall
University of Minnesota
Minneapolis, MN 55420
March 15, 1984

Caroline Levine
Vice-President of Advertising
  & Marketing
Kansas City Federal Savings
1543 Grove Avenue
Kansas City, MO 64132

Dear Mrs. Levine:
According to the United States Savings League, the rate of
savings is going down, and the competition for the savings
dollar from banks, thrifts and loans, brokerage houses, and now
mass-merchandisers like Sears and American Express has never
been greater.

I realize this must be a major concern for you, and I have read
that you are currently expanding your department and mounting
an aggressive campaign to counteract this competition. This is
the kind of project I could really sink my teeth into. Generating
new ideas and implementing them is what I like doing best, and I
would like to direct my energies toward the fields of advertising
and marketing.

In fact, since my background is in art -- I am graduating as an
art major from the University of Minnesota in June -- I have
developed some advertising materials for your campaign that I
would like to present to you. I am terribly excited by them and
I am hoping they are an effective way to get your message across.
I look forward to meeting with you to discuss this further. I
will call you on March 26th, to see if a meeting can be arranged.

Sincerely yours,

Sandra Kuczek
Sandra Kuczek

126 Grant Avenue
Tyler, TX 75702
April 4, 1984

Lionel Bauman
Director of Sales
Hi-Tech Inc.
1000 Circle Drive
Austin, TX 78745

Dear Mr. Bauman:
    The competition in the personal computer market has never
been stronger. With the Apple II, the Atari 800, and the IBM
Personal Computer 5150 competing against your 1500 model, I
would guess it is somewhat difficult to penetrate the market
the way you would like to.

    That's why you must need aggressive salespeople who know
your product to represent you. Mr. Bauman, I believe I may be
just the person you are looking for. I have owned your 1500
model for the last year, and I am convinced it is far superior
to the products of your competitors, and I would like to tell you
why. In addition, I have an excellent personality for sales and
a history of achievement. When I was membership chairman of the
campus chess club, membership rose by 25 percent. When I was
captain of our intramural baseball team, we won the championship.
When I worked in a local department store during the Christmas
season, sales were up 10 percent from the previous year.

    What I would like to do now is turn my energies toward selling
your computers. I'm familiar with your product line. I like what
I've read about your company. And I would like very much to discuss a future relationship. Since it is difficult to reach me
by telephone, I will call you on Wednesday, April 18th, to see
when an appointment can be arranged.

                                        Sincerely yours,

                                        Peter Sykes

                                        Peter Sykes

The follow-up

Once you've specified in your letter that you plan to call on a designated day, be sure you do it. It suggests the ability to follow through and an attention to detail. You can usually expect the following scenario:

Secretary: "Hello, Lionel Bauman's office."

Pete: "Hello, this is Pete Sykes. I sent Mr. Bauman a letter on April 4th, and I'm calling to set up an appointment to discuss it further."

At this point, there are a few possible scenarios. One is that the secretary has either been instructed to make the appointment with you, or to tell you her boss is not interested in meeting with you. This is the easiest to deal with because you know where you stand immediately. This is rare. A second possibility is that she has been given no instructions, but that she remembers your letter since one of her jobs is to open the mail. This is rare, but not unheard of. The third, and most likely, is that she has been given no instructions and doesn't remember your letter. In that case, she will probably say, "Mr. Bauman is in a meeting right now. May I ask you what this is regarding?"

Your immediate response is to say, "It's regarding a job."

Bite your tongue because you don't want her to say, "I'm sorry. We're not hiring now." That's a typical response, and what she's trying to do is to protect her boss from the hordes of job-seekers who call daily. It would be better for you to refer to your original letter so she knows once again that you've written to her boss, and that perhaps he is interested in meeting with you.

Pete: "As I mentioned in my letter of April 4th, I would like to arrange a meeting to discuss the ideas I outlined in my letter. Can you tell me when he'll be available, or may I set up an appointment with you?"

Secretary: "He'll be in and out all day, and I will have to confirm the appointment with him. May I take a number where you can be reached?"

130

Pete:	"My number is 872-2024, but since I have a number of other appointments today, I think it would probably be better for me to call him this afternoon. Would 3 o'clock be a convenient time?"
Secretary:	"Yes, it would."
Pete:	"Thank you, and what is your name?"
Secretary:	"Shirley."
Pete:	"I appreciate your help, Shirley, and I will talk to you at 3 o'clock."

What's important to learn is that it's best to enlist the aid of the secretary in trying to arrange an appointment. It is difficult, if not impossible, to circumvent the involvement of the secretary in your business. It's best to get the secretary on your team by including her in the appointment-making process. After all, the job of a good secretary is to screen out those calls that her boss would not want to take, or at very least, to find out what the nature of the calls are. If you enlist her aid by explaining the nature of the call up-front and by asking her when a good time to call back is, it's a far more productive process, even though it will probably still have some frustrating moments.

When you call back the first time, it is quite possible that she won't have a meeting time set up for you. Either she wasn't able to discuss it with her boss, or her boss didn't give her an answer. Again, enlist her aid in coming up with another time to call back. By now, you will have spoken to each other a number of times, and she will probably make the extra effort to make sure you get that appointment, if she likes you and if she can. On the other hand, it doesn't always work out that way.

Secretary:	"Hello, Lionel Bauman's office."
Pete:	"Hello, Shirley? This is Pete Sykes. We spoke this morning. I called regarding the sales ideas that I'd like to discuss with Mr. Bauman. Were you able to set up a meeting?"

Secretary: "No, Pete, I'm sorry I wasn't. I do have your number, and I will try to call you tomorrow morning."

Pete: "I have a number of other meetings tomorrow. So why don't I call you back? Is this a good time?"

Secretary: "Yes, it is."

Pete: "Good. I'll call you at 3 o'clock then. Thank you, Shirley."

Secretary: "Good-bye, Pete."

When you call back the next day at 3 o'clock, it is still quite possible that you won't get an appointment. After all, you are not Shirley's boss' top priority, and he may have other things on his mind, like running his business. On the other hand, you're already a couple of steps ahead of the game: you and Shirley are on a first-name basis, and she knows you are a person of your word because you always call when you say you will. Chances are, if you continue to be polite but persistent, Shirley will eventually help to arrange an appointment for you on the phone, if she can.

[Sometimes a secretary can't, as was the case with Joyce, the secretary for a news director at a local radio station. I called Joyce for five days straight, and she would always say her boss, Peter Jaffe, was in a meeting. She was very professional about it, but very cold, and I couldn't seem to break the veneer. At the end of five days, I was getting frustrated, and I almost decided that no job was worth the aggravation. On the other hand, I wasn't a quitter by nature. When I looked at the problem rationally, I realized that it wasn't all that bleak. Even though she hadn't made an appointment for me, she also hadn't told me to stop calling. Perhaps all I needed was a different approach. Maybe the phone technique didn't work for everyone...

[The alternative was obvious. I arrived at the station at 10 o'clock the next morning. When the guard at the entrance asked me who I was there to see and whether I was expected, I said, "I'm here to see Mr. Jaffe and I do not have an appointment." He looked at me expectantly. I continued, "Mr. Jaffe is always in meetings when I call, so I decided that perhaps he could see me between his meetings." This time the guard looked at me as if I'd just arrived from the backwoods country. He called Joyce, who came right down...

[I introduced myself, and told her what a pleasure it was to meet her since we had spoken so many times on the phone. I repeated what I had said to the guard about Mr. Jaffe being in meetings. I told her that I was hoping to catch him between meetings. She was quite surprised to see me, and told me to call her at 2 o'clock that afternoon. I did and she set up an appointment for me the next day...

[The meeting was anti-climactic. Mr. Jaffe didn't have a job for me, and that's why he didn't return my calls. But I learned an important lesson. What I learned was that you can generally get what you want if you're willing to persevere. The point to make here is that the best direct contact sales letter means nothing if you can't get in the door. So, your follow-up must be as creative as your approach. — *Susan Bernard.*]

The direct contact approach, like the traditional sources approach, is just another method of trying to generate interviews. It should be used in conjunction with other techniques, rather than as a replacement for other techniques. Sometimes a direct contact campaign will work successfully for you; sometimes it won't. Once again, the more letters you send out and the more leads you pursue, the greater your possibility of success will be. And once again, if a particular type of letter and campaign is not working for you, find out why. Show your letter to someone whose opinion you respect. Ask them how they would respond. Show it to a career counselor at school and get their opinion. Send a copy to the president of the industry trade association and ask for their advice. Your skills in utilizing this approach, like all of the others, is dependent on these variables: your ability to create an effective campaign, your capacity of learning from your mistakes, and your willingness to persevere in the face of rejection.

9

Interview Enthusiastically

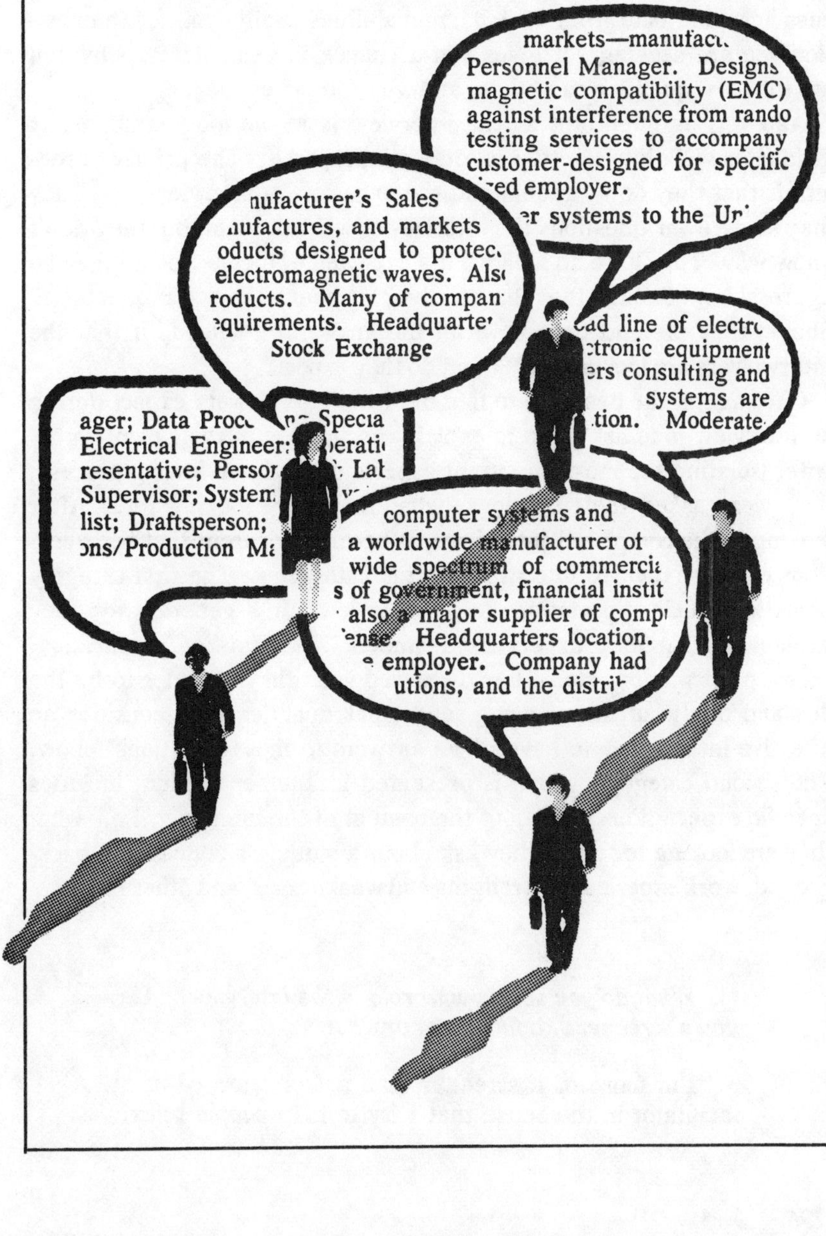

Since all the preparation, planning, library research, resume writing, and field research you've done so far had been carried out so that you can target a career and then set up the appropriate job search interviews, it is obvious how important the interview is in the job search process. It is your opportunity to sell yourself to a company. It is an occasion for you to explain yourself to a company. It allows you to discuss how your background, skills, and abilities qualify you for the position you are seeking. It gives you a chance to demonstrate why you are the most qualified candidate, and why you can do the job.

And yet, as important as the interview is in the job search, many graduates walk into interviews totally unprepared. The primary problem is that they don't understand the dynamics of interviewing. They may know *what* questions the interviewer will ask them, but they don't know *why*. They have no idea what's expected of them. Should they be aggressive? Should they be passive? Should they ask questions? Should they pretend they have all the answers? What is it that the interviewers are looking for? What do they expect?

Once again, the best way to find out what interviewers expect during an interview is to ask them to explain the process in their own words. After isolating the most important aspects of the interviewing process, they were asked their opinions; what they were looking for. After looking at the completed interviews, it became apparent that the questions could be divided into two different categories. The first category deals with their expectations in an interview. In a general way, they explained what they expect from students in terms of preparation, dress, participation, etc. They discussed what they consider to be the dos and don'ts of interviewing, and what qualities they consider an effective interviewee to have. The answers to those questions follow. The second category, which is presented in another section, includes specific expectations regarding the content of the interview, i.e., what they are looking for when they ask about a student's educational background, work experience, strengths and weaknesses, and other factors.

Q: What do you see as your role in the interview? Are you a screener or a facilitator or what?

"I'm more of a screener than a facilitator. I'm a facilitator in the sense that I try to help people relax, especially in a panel. I've been through it myself to know how difficult it can be. My primary role, however, is as a screener."

Marilyn M. Lurie
Assistant Director
Community Development Division
City of Los Angeles

"I think in any interview you have to be a screener, but I don't believe in a set program of what I call 'personnel-type' questions that any student who's had more than two interviews has stock answers for. I think the most effective way to learn about candidates is to find out what kind of questions they have. By soliciting questions, you find out what they know about you, about the company, what their interest level is, and you begin to find out about them. It's a good jumping off place."

Charles A. Buck Jr.
Senior Vice-President
Director of Administrative Services
BBDO International, Inc.

"I see myself as both. The job is to screen out the good ones from the average ones. It's also our job to excite the person about our company. Whether or not we pursue a person, we want all people to be excited about our company. In an interview, we try to differentiate those who would fit in well with our company, and to give out information about our company."

Lee A. Junkans
Administrator of College Relations
Eaton Corporation

"As a campus recruiter, I have a dual role: to select highly qualified candidates for further consideration, and to convey to all applicants a favorable impression of our firm. I see both roles as important."

Brian J. Farrell
Supervisor
Deloitte Haskins & Sells

Q: What are the most common problems that students have in an interview?

"Not knowing what they're applying for. Not researching the organization. Bad communication skills that run the gamut from a lack of eye contact to the constant usage of 'you know'. An indication that they haven't really thought about the questions that an interviewer will ask. A lack of preparation."

Gordon T. Hill
Manager/College Relations
First Interstate Bank

"An inability to establish rapport, to speak effectively, to sustain a conversation."

John L. Massingale
Personnel Manager
Touche Ross & Company

"They don't research the organization. Let me give you an example. Some students will apply for a job in our company in an area where we don't have a plant or facility. So we reject them, and large companies like Mobil don't have time to explain to everyone why we're rejecting them. We just send a form letter. Some students come in without knowing anything about themselves. They haven't thought about their interests and their skills. With our company, there are people jobs, analytical jobs, and jobs that encompass both people and analysis. Students should know what they like doing and what they're able to do. Instead, they try to make themselves qualified for anything, but they shouldn't do that. You need to state what you're good at. There's nobody who's equally good in everything."

Verna G. Bennett
Regional Recruiting Coordinator
Mobil Oil

Q: What is the importance of clothes in getting a job?

"It's part of an appearance that's essential. They should be exceedingly neat. The way they look in the

138

interview is the way they'll look at my company."

Mark Guterman
Manager of Human Resource Planning
Mervyn's Stores

"They play an average role. The only time I remember getting turned off is when I had a student wearing a corduroy suit with matching running shoes. Later, when I met one of his professors on campus, the guy was wearing the same outfit. I guess the student used him as a role model."

John L. Massingale
Personnel Manager
Touche Ross & Company

"I'm laughing because I'm thinking of all the articles on dressing for success. I think that clothes are important. I mean, clothes make a statement of what you are. If someone comes into an interview in a pair of Levis and a crew neck sweater, which would look perfectly fine out of an office environment, I think it says something to you. I don't find that people do that, though. I think young men should wear suits or a blazer or a sports jacket. I think a suit is more appropriate probably, generally speaking. I think a woman should wear a suit or a skirt and blouse — something that shows that she's serious and understands that clothing makes a difference. There's no question about it."

Charles A. Buck Jr.
Senior Vice-President
Director of Administrative Services
BBDO International, Inc.

Q: From your experience, are there any dos and don'ts that you can recommend to an interviewee?

"Do ask questions. A lot of people just respond to what you ask them. They never initiate any questions themselves. Asking questions indicates an interest in the job. A person who asks questions in an interview also shows me that they will ask questions if they work for mc. That's good. It's a sign of initiative. It shows they're secure. Look for clues in an interview. You should be able to tell by the interviewer's response whether you're talking too long or whether you should stop asking questions. If the interviewer is looking at her watch or fidgeting in her chair, it's time to stop talking..."

Marilyn M. Lurie
Assistant Director
Community Development Division
City of Los Angeles

"Think through the potential questions, particularly as they relate to your background. Be prepared. Questions like, 'What kind of firm are you?' demonstrate a lack of preparation and knowledge. You should know who you are and be prepared to express your personal goals."

John L. Massingale
Personnel Manager
Touche Ross & Company

Q: How do you distinguish between an average interviewee and a star?

"For me, it's very intuitive. I interview in a non-structured and intuitive way, but I can tell the stars at the beginning. It starts the moment they open the door. From their handshake to when they leave. It's a positive attitude. It's the way they answer questions."

Mark Guterman
Manager of Human Resource Planning
Mervyn's Stores

"You just feel it when it's happening. Their answers are ready. They're concise. They have a sense of the position they're interviewing for. They've thought about their background. They have the ability to think on their feet. They're enthusiastic. They talk with some degree of excitement, with animation. Other people talk and you want to fall asleep."

Marilyn M. Lurie
Assistant Director
Community Development Division
City of Los Angeles

"A star radiates. A star has a magic ability. Within 15 minutes you can tell if someone is a star. They have self-confidence. They have an understanding of people. A star knows what they want. They focus on it. They are pleasant to be with. They know what they want and they know how to get it."

Daniel S. Goldin
Manager of Communication Systems Projects
TRW Electronics & Defense

As you can see, the interviewers may differ on specifics, but a few things are quite clear: they expect you to be prepared for interviews. They expect you to play an active role. They expect you to be able to communicate. And in order to be able to do any of that, you've got to understand the basics of interviewing, which follow.

THE PURPOSE

The purpose of a job interview is to sell yourself. You've got to let the interviewer know that your background, your skills, and your abilities are absolutely right for the job. In order to accomplish this goal, you've got to exchange information. You will learn about the job, company, and industry; an employer will learn about you, about your background, about your goals. However, a lot of that will be done in the preparatory phase. You'll learn much of the objective information about the organization from their annual report and other printed materials. They will find out about your qualifications from your resume. Employers generally only interview people who they know can do the job. Certainly, completing a bachelor's degree indicates you have the potential for almost any job. The interview allows an employer to observe you. It allows you to observe the employer. Indeed, the interview is a two-way street. And that is the point. The interview is an information exchange with each party having an equal role.

WHAT TO EXPECT

Generally, for each job you can expect a minimum of two interviews of 45-60 minutes each. The screening interview, conducted by a personnel specialist, will determine if you meet the general characteristics for the position and the organization. The hiring interview, conducted by a line manager or supervisor — the person you will work for — will judge your technical qualifications for the job. In a small company, the screening and hiring interviews may be one and the same, conducted by the same person. On the other hand, the hiring interview in a large organization may be conducted by a series of people — near peers, and more senior management, or a panel of interviewers.

Don't panic. The rules are the same. There are structured interviews in which you will be asked a standard set of questions in a more or less prescribed order. There are unstructured interviews in which the interviewer pursues whatever line of questioning seems appropriate.

HOW TO PREPARE

Careful preparation will give you more confidence and boost your overall performance and will, therefore, give you the edge over your competition. You must prepare for each interview separately, using a job at a particular company as the parameter within which you will frame your response. Your preparation will fall into two familiar categories: self-assessment, and labor market research.

Self-assessment

Sit down with your resume and think about what you want to stress in the interview. If you left out some information from your resume that seems to have an application for a particular job, make note of it. Develop a clear understanding of your education and experience, and their value to you and to an employer. Identify your skills, abilities, and interests in such terms as intelligence, creativity, leadership qualities, motivation, communication skills, interpersonal skills, and technical skills. Be prepared to cite examples that will bring these qualities to light. Analyze your strengths and weaknesses, personal aspirations and goals, values and attitudes, and expectations. Pay attention to your accomplishments and how you may relate them in a specific situation.

Labor market research

Once again, this part of the process is where you gather information about the job and the organization. Many of you will have already completed this research way before you set up an interview. You've either done it when you were interviewing for information, or perhaps when you wrote a letter to a direct contact. But if you haven't, it's crucial that you do it now.

The most effective way to proceed is to start out by gathering generalized, unbiased information from standard library resources. Then read the company-produced information, and complete the process by talking to people in the field. This preparation need not take days. A little preparation goes a long way, if it's the right kind.

In order to find out as much as you can about the particular position for which you are applying, start with a general publication about careers, such as the *Dictionary of Occupational Titles,* a publication of the U.S. Department of Labor which can be found in the reference section of most libraries. This publication *(DOT)* gives general job descriptions that include all the possible duties ever performed in that job category. An actual job will differ in that all the duties will rarely be included and a priority of tasks will be expected. But you need some generalized idea of what the job will encompass before you walk in the door, so you don't sound like a moron in the interview. It is obviously far more impressive to ask an interviewer questions like, "Which functions are given priority in this job?", or, "Will I be spending more of my time making cold calls on the phone, or in the field?", than it is to say, "What does a salesperson do?"

Once you've learned about the job, learn about the company. Start with their annual report and also consult other published literature: directories such as *Standard & Poor's Register of Corporations, Directors, and Executives,* and current periodicals such as *Business Week, Fortune, Venture, Inc.,* and many others. These magazines will give you insight into the organization's most recent activities, including new products or services, new directions, or problems. Also read trade publications.

You may also want to talk to people you know — particularly if they are in a related field — who may have information about the company or the person you're interviewing with. Personal contacts may yield details not available in the library, such as the actual working environment, turnover rate of personnel, and reputation.

Specific information you will want to have includes the size of the organization, its divisions and subsidiaries and where they are located, the structure of its departments, the age of the company, its past and its future. Current problems and needs may be more difficult to identify, but will be valuable data for the interview.

Your research should center on relating the information about a job and a company to your own experience. You need to be able to answer the following questions in an interview: "Why do you want to work for this company? What do you know about the job? The company? The industry? What interests you about the products or services the company offers? Why do you think you would like this job? How does this job fit into your long-term goals?"

Salary

Think about your salary expectations and decide on an acceptable range. Professional salaries are normally stated in monthly or annual figures. Know the exceptions. You will want to know what to expect. Research current salaries for your field. There are Department of Labor studies, professional association projections, and the salaries included for similar positions in the want-ads. The best source is the College Placement Council's annual salary survey. Your college placement office will have a copy.

Dressing for success

Another part of the preparation involves your appearance. Dress is *very* important, and should be attended to well before the interview. Decide what you're going to wear. Avoid extremes in appearance, and dress appropriately for the particular work setting. Err on the side of being conservative. You will not offend anyone if you wear a business suit; you may seriously hamper your chances for a job if you wear inappropriate clothes.

For men, a well-tailored, dark suit, conservative shirt, and tie are generally acceptable. Excessive facial hair and long hair produce strong negative reactions. For women, a well-tailored suit and blouse or a conservative dress are favored. Pantsuits are not acceptable. Short skirts, low necklines, trendy outfits, and excessive makeup create negative impressions.

Miscellaneous preparation

Know the location of the company and the best travel arrangements *before* the morning of your interview. If you will be driving, make sure you have access to a reliable car on the days you've scheduled interviews. Leave early so you have sufficient time to relax and mentally review what you plan to say. Punctuality is critical.

THE CONTENT

A typical interview consists of three segments: the ice-breaking period, which usually sets the tone of the interview; the body of the interview, in which there is an exchange of information; and the closing, which establishes what will happen as a result of the interview. The follow-up, which is in effect the fourth segment, occurs after the interview has been completed.

The ice-breaking period

This is the first three to five minutes of the interview. You've been introduced to the interviewer. You either shook hands or you didn't. You've quickly looked him over to see what he's wearing. He's done the same with you. You sit down. There's a moment of silence. What do you do? Should you talk? Will he?

Q: What do you expect from the interviewee in the ice-breaking period?

"A lot of nervousness. Courtesy. Eye contact. Answers to my questions. I expect that people will assert themselves early on. Undergraduates are typically bad at that. They let me control the interview. Sometimes I ask an open-ended question to see how they respond. I give them the opportunity to say what they want."

Mark Guterman
Manager of Human Resource Planning
Mervyn's Stores

"Job applicants should respond to the ice-breaking. They should not always wait for me to ask the next question. That suggests a certain passivity."

Brian J. Farrell
Supervisor
Deloitte Haskins & Sells

"Sometimes as an interviewer, my day has been rotten. My mind is on many other problems. Sometimes it's helpful if they try to ease things. That requires a certain flexibility. If I'm up, then I'll go out of my way to make them feel at ease. If I'm not, they need to sense the situation. They've got to be sensitive to my needs."

Daniel S. Goldin
Manager of Communication Systems Projects
TRW Electronics & Defense

"I hope they can demonstrate a certain security and comfort with themselves. It's an uncomfortable time for both parties, so it's important to get started on the right foot. I look for alertness, too. Don't wait for the interviewer to take the lead."

Jan Stein
Director of Personnel & Training
American Heart Association

"Probably the ability to be themselves, to have the poise to move right into the conversation. It will show that they can deal effectively with clients. An ability to establish rapport."

John L. Massingale
Personnel Manager
Touche Ross & Company

The body

The body of the interview should be an information exchange. It should be where the interviewer tells you about his company, and asks you questions about yourself. It should also be where you volunteer pertinent information that he hasn't asked you about, and ask him questions you need answers to. For most graduates, however, the interviewer's questions comprise the majority of the interview, so that's a good place to begin. The following is a list of the 15 most commonly-asked interview questions.

1. Why did you choose your academic major?

2. What courses did you like best? Least? Why?

3. What kind of extra-curricular activities were you involved with?

4. What kind of job are you interested in?

5. How did your college career prepare you for this type of work?

6. Have you had summer or previous employment in this or a related field?

7. What have you learned from your work experience?

8. Why are you interviewing with our company?

9. What are the most important considerations for you in choosing a job?

10. What do you see yourself doing five years from now? Ten years from now?

11. What do you do in your leisure time?

12. What are your strengths and weaknesses?

13. What are your ideas on salary?

14. Why should we hire you?

15. Do you have any questions?

How should you respond to these questions? What do employers want to know? Let's take a look.

Q: What are you looking for in an interview when the job-seeker talks about his educational background?

"We're looking for pertinent accounting courses. We're looking for an overall measure of academic success, which would have to be their GPA."

John L. Massingale
Personnel Manager
Touche Ross & Company

"I'd rather have a liberal arts background. I think a liberal arts student is a more flexible student; they don't become entangled with technicalities. If you understand the humanities, the classics, you can move from there to anything. I look at what they've done at school and what they've done on the outside at the same time."

Paul F. Mahoney
Vice-President
New York Life Insurance Company

"Factual information. Their degree, their program, school, GPA. Under what conditions was the degree attained? What commitment did the individual evidence by attaining a degree. I'm very interested in GPA. It's an excellent indicator of an individual's discipline. It shows an ability to stick to a goal. It shows that they are bright people with capacity."

David Mitchell
Manager/Marketing & Service Support
Xerox Corporation

"Self-intuition. Thinking. Motivation. What drives them. What's important to them."

Verna G. Bennett
Regional Recruiting Coordinator
Mobil Oil Corporation

Q: What do you look for when someone talks about their work experience?

"What they have learned from it, what did they 'take home', but not the overly specific or technical aspects of the job. Did the person work in groups? Did anyone report to them? No matter what the job, they must have learned something positive. Remember, the recruiter has to sell management on hiring their selected candidates, so the graduate must give the recruiter some information to work with. For example, if you spent four summers selling rugs, we need to know what positive things you learned about yourself while selling rugs.''

Bruce J. Eswein II
Personnel Manager of
Executive Recruitment & Development
BBDO International, Inc.

''I'm looking for people that have some involvement with people. We're people oriented. Just the fact that somebody has worked says something. If they worked in a human resources program rather than at a resort, it says something, too...It's also how they explain what they've done. It's how they perceive their experience. Not just paid work experience. I look for some example that the individual has some commitment to something. That they've had a responsibility of putting together a special function. It's a clue that they've had exposure to things not going the way they're supposed to. It demonstrates that they've used planning and organizing skills.''

Marilyn M. Lurie
Assistant Director
Community Development Division
City of Los Angeles

''I'm looking to see if their exposure has been similar to what it's going to be in our environment. What have they achieved? What kinds of problems did they face, and how did they solve them?''

Lee A. Junkans
Administrator of College Relations
Eaton Corporation

''I don't care what their jobs have been, but I want to see if they've learned anything from working. I'm interested in how they relate to work. Are they responsible? What is it going to mean to them? How does

149

work affect their self-esteem?"

Mark Guterman
Manager of Human Resource Planning
Mervyn's Stores

Q: What are you looking for when you ask a student about their strengths and weaknesses?

"I primarily ask about their strengths. Do they demonstrate initiative, determination, and organization? I even look for a bit of competitive aggressiveness."

Gordon T. Hill
Manager/College Relations
First Interstate Bank

"I look at the type of things they say. When they discuss weaknesses, I like to see that they have an understanding of themselves. In terms of strengths, I look at the kind of things that make them proud."

Brian J. Farrell
Supervisor
Deloitte Haskins & Sells

"To see how candid they are. To see if they can make a good self-appraisal. To know one's strengths and weaknesses indicates a sense of maturity."

Daniel S. Goldin
Manager of Communications Systems Projects
TRW Electronics & Defense

Q: Who should initiate questions about salary and when?

"The students should initiate it on a plant tour. Engineering is an exception. They've usually got some work experience. If a student wants to know about salaries in the industry, they can check with their placement center. We have salary ranges and salary groups. That should be part of their research. In an interview, if they start talking about money right away, you begin to think that money is their top priority, and starting salary is not that important. You can start low and end up high; but you're never told that."

Verna G. Bennett
Regional Recruiting Coordinator
Mobil Oil Corporation

"I like to initiate that myself. Generally speaking, there's a fixed salary level for undergraduates...There really isn't any good time in an interview for them to ask about it. If they ask in the middle, it can break up the flow of an interview. If they ask at the end, that may be what the interviewer remembers when he's filling out the evaluation."

Gordon T. Hill
Manager/College Relations
First Interstate Bank

"I think the interviewer should initiate questions about salary when he or she thinks it appropriate. When I'm talking to an experienced executive, I'll ask them pretty much at the beginning of an interview how much money he or she is looking for. With a student, I don't think the question of salary should really come up. Most places are going to pay fairly competitive salaries for beginners. There are norms that they can check with to see what salaries are."

Charles A. Buck Jr.
Senior Vice-President
Director of Administrative Services
BBDO International, Inc.

Once again, employers may differ on the specifics. There is obviously no right or wrong answer. It depends on the interviewer, the job, the company, and the industry. However, there are some guidelines that have an overall application.

Guidelines
Be sure you hear the question, understand the question, and answer

the question. If the question is not clear to you, ask for clarification. Restate the question if necessary. Listening to the interviewer is also essential. It helps to know what is *said* and what is *meant*. You may not always be able to distinguish the difference. Careful listening will allow you to understand the question, not what you *think* the question is.

In answering questions, pause to give yourself time to compose an answer that is concise and thoughtful. Elaborate briefly on your applicable skills and related education and experience. Give examples whenever possible. Be specific. Be positive. In order to maintain the interviewer's focus on objective factors, you need to discuss special qualifications for the position several times during the interview, mentioning specific skills and related education and experience. What will be remembered are specific examples, not general concepts. Don't hesitate to be the initiator. Introduce information if you think it's important. Essentially, your job in the interview is to fill in between the lines of your resume. How does your previous experience relate to the job? How did your education prepare you for this job?

Asking questions

Ask questions if you need information. The questions you ask should not be those you should have already researched. Asking about the size of a company, where its headquarters are, what product it sells, and what the job you're applying for encompasses are *not* good questions. Good questions indicate you're aware of those variables. Good questions suggest you've done your homework. The difference between poorly-developed questions and well thought-out questions may be the difference between getting a job and not getting one.

To give some examples: you should *not* ask, "What products do you produce?" You might ask, "Are there plans to develop a new product line?" You should *not* ask, "Tell me about the job." You might ask, "How much of my time will be spent in writing and research as opposed to community involvement?" You should *not* ask, "When will I get promoted?" You might ask, "What is the typical upward mobility of someone who comes to this company with my background?" In other words, you should not ask questions that are obvious or that you might have found answers to if you had done a little research. You *should* ask questions that demonstrate at least a basic knowledge of the job, occupation, and company.

The summary and closing

This is the last part of the interview, and it usually establishes the next step. After a positive concluding statement, such as, "Mr. Smith, I am convinced — now more than ever — that my skills and my background would be right for this position, and I would really like the job," you should find out when the decision will be made. Will there be another interview, and when? How soon can you expect to hear from them? Can you call to follow up? When? Who?

The follow-up

This step follows the interview and can be very important, if properly utilized. The follow-up is comprised of two different elements: the evaluation, and the thank-you letter.

The evaluation is the where you sit down and analyze the interview. Before you begin, you need to ask yourself whether you want the job you applied for. If not, make sure you understand why. Is it the company you don't want to work for? Is is the industry? Is it the interviewer? Is it the wrong job? If so, why? What elements don't you like? What elements do you like? What did you learn about yourself that will help you target a job that you'll like better?

On the other hand, if you *do* want the job, did you sell yourself well? Does the interviewer know why you're a capable candidate? Did you relate your skills to the position you're seeking? Did you evidence an understanding of what the job encompasses, and did you explain why you could do a good job? Were you enthusiastic? Did you demonstrate your interest? Did you ask for the job?

Whatever you did or did not do, make note of it — there's always room for improvement — but also realize that "the opera isn't over until the fat lady sings." In other words, you still have one more opportunity to sell yourself; to convince the employer that you're the right person for the position. That's the thank-you letter, which is the second element of the follow-up.

Gene Ross, Director of Recruitment & Placement at Bullock's, best describes the value of the thank-you letter.

"A lot of people don't send one," he said. "Those who do, it's noticed. I think it's a good thing, and if you can say something more than 'thank you' in the note — something more than a banality of some kind — it can make it more meaningful. If someone is on the fence about you, maybe a well-written thank-you note will make them think about

(text continues on page 155)

THE INTERVIEW

Dos
- Research the job and company thoroughly.
- Act natural and appear relaxed.
- Show enthusiasm.
- Listen to the interviewer.
- Clarify ambiguous questions.
- Know yourself — interests, skills, strengths, weaknesses, and goals.
- Give specific examples to support your statements.
- Ask relevant questions.
- Summarize the main points at the end of the interview.
- Clarify follow-up procedures.

Don'ts
- Be late.
- Present an extreme appearance.
- Become emotional.
- Talk too much.
- Talk too little.
- Be vague.
- Oversell your case.
- Try to be funny.
- Overemphasize salary and benefits.
- Criticize yourself or undervalue your background.

you again, and consider you further.''

What's important to remember from this statement is *"that it's a good thing if you can say something more than 'thank you.'"* The authors of this book agree. Think of the thank-you letter as another sales letter. What you're trying to do is close the deal. A good thank-you letter will tell the interviewer something he doesn't already know about you. You might tell him what you learned in the interview. You might relate your skills more clearly to the position you're seeking. You might tell him how excited you are about his company and why you want to work there. A good sales thank-you letter, such as the following ones, should excite the reader.

836 East 48th Street
New York, NY 10067

May 21, 1984

Frank Taylor
Sales Manager
XYZ Copier Company
1536 Avenue of the Americas
New York, NY 10024

Dear Mr. Taylor:
   Thank you so much for meeting with me yesterday. I am excited
about the possibility of selling your product.

   After listening to your analysis of the market, I am convinced --
more than ever -- that there's an enormous sales potential, and
I think my background would be a real asset to you.

   My sales experience at Bloomingdale's is strong. As I mentioned
in our interview, I was the top performer during the last two
Christmas seasons. My knowledge of the copier industry is increasing
daily. After our meeting, I spent the rest of the afternoon checking
out the competitive products, and I am beginning to get a real
handle on why your product is different; how it's better.

   Most importantly, I want you to know I am a real achiever. I've
always succeeded at whatever I've done. As you know, I excelled at
tennis at NYU. While serving as membership chairperson at my sorority,
we had more applicants than ever before. My GPA is strong, even though
I worked to support myself through college.

   Mr. Taylor, I am convinced I could make a valuable contribution
to XYZ Copier Company. I hope you agree. I will call you next week
to see if we can discuss this further.

                              Sincerely,

                              Mary Sullivan
                              Mary Sullivan

1535 East 53rd Street
Chicago, IL 60615

June 27, 1984

Janet Dowd
Director of Social Services
St. Joseph's Hospital
1234 Main Street
Chicago, IL 60636

Dear Ms. Dowd:
I enjoyed meeting with you last week to discuss the exciting
opportunity in the play therapy program. St. Joseph's Hospital
has certainly taken the lead in this important area, and I
would be pleased to be associated with the program.

Our conversation further convinced me that a good match exists
between my background and your expectations for the job. In
addition to my major in Psychology at DePaul University and the
experience I have had in Program Development for the Chicago
Department of Parks and Recreation, I would like to emphasize my
participation in the project with Dr. Stein at Michael Reese
Hospital. It provided me with insight into using dance as an
effective mode of expression with certain groups of children --
a concept I would like to develop further in the program at St.
Joseph's.

I look forward to hearing from you soon. I will contact you by
Friday if you are unable to reach me before then.

Sincerely,

Judy Fried
Judy Fried

1066 Third Street
Cape Coral, FL 33904
July 15, 1984

Barbara Galvan
Vice-President
Human Resources Department
Avery Helicopter Corporation
789 State Street
Ft. Lauderdale, FL 33916

Dear Ms. Galvan:

Our interview yesterday confirmed my commitment to Human Resources as the most vital area within business today. The position as an employment interviewer for Avery would combine my interest in working with people and my background in engineering technology. I was surprised and delighted to find you have a similar background. And I was pleased to find that Avery Helicopter Corporation appreciates this combination.

I look forward to my second interview with John Lansing next Wednesday. I will let you know how it turns out. Once again, I appreciate your efforts on my behalf.

Sincerely,

Joe Donovan
Joe Donovan

As you can tell, each of these letters is highly individualized, and is tailored to the company, the industry, and the person with whom the student interviewed. That's as it should be. Once again, the thank-you letter may be your last opportunity to explain how your background will meet an employer's needs. It is an important selling tool if you understand its function.

Some general guidelines are appropriate. Be sure to write the thank-you letter promptly, while the interview is still fresh in your mind. In the letter, refer to specific points discussed, or highlight facts about your background that are pertinent to the position you're seeking, and which will set you apart from other candidates. Be specific. The thank-you letter is your opportunity to add any information in support of your application that you may have neglected to mention in the interview. Use it well!

Evaluate Your Offers

Managing an effective job search campaign is a difficult task at any stage in your life. It seems most difficult when you are just graduating from college. All of a sudden, you're suddenly thrust into a situation you are seemingly unprepared for. You feel great about finally getting your degree until you approach the marketplace. Suddenly it's not that easy. Actually, it's not that difficult either. When you think about it, there are only two eventualities: rejection, or success.

DEALING WITH SUCCESS

At some point in your job search, someone will make you an offer. The optimum, of course, is that after you have been on a good number of interviews, you are offered a half-dozen jobs, and you have to choose from among them. Wouldn't that be wonderful? Chances are, however, that unless you are an engineer or a business major from one of the most prestigious schools who was student body president, graduated Phi Beta Kappa, and worked on internships every summer, that won't be the case. What is more realistic is that you will be offered at least two jobs, and you will have to make a decision between them.

Suddenly, you're scared to death. What if you make the wrong decision? What if you pick the wrong job? How can you tell which company is truly the best place to work?

If you share any of these feelings, rest assured — you're in good company. Most recent graduates find the decision-making process somewhat difficult. Once again, they're suddenly afraid they may make the wrong choice. What they don't realize is that *no* choice is irreversible. If a company offers you a job today and you refuse it — but you deal with them in a professional manner — chances are they might be interested in you two years down the road. Be that as it may, it is obviously a good idea to choose as wisely as possible.

The best method for doing this consists of two elements: you need to identify factors that are important to you, and you need to prioritize them. The most important factors, originally introduced by personnel specialist James B. Morris (and since refined and adapted by the authors of this book) follow:

1. *Location.* Is the company located in an area where you want to live and work? Will the cultural, educational, and social opportunities meet your needs? Where do they have other branches, divisions, or operations? Will you have to move if you get promoted? Is that location agreeable?

162

2. *Location for Spouse's Career.*   Can your spouse get a job in this geographic area? Is this a priority?

3. *Travel.*   How much of your time will be spent traveling, whether it's local, national, or international? How do you feel about this?

4. *Salary.*   How much money will you be paid on a yearly basis? When will you be evaluated for an increase? What kind of increase can you expect?

5. *Benefits.*   What does the complete compensation package include? How many days of vacation? What types of insurance coverage do they offer?

6. *Training Programs.*   Do you want to participate in a rotational training program that provides broad exposure? Will you be able to concentrate on specific training in one area? Which avenue do you prefer?

7. *Learning Potential.*   What is the extent and rate at which your understanding of the job and company will develop? How long can you remain in the job without feeling you've outgrown it?

8. *Significant Responsibility.*   When can you have impact on the way your division or department is being run? Will you have high visibility right away? Is that something you want?

9. *Variety of Work.*   Will the job encompass a variety of unrelated tasks, or will you be responsible for one primary function? How important is diversity to you?

10. *Job Status.*   How is your job viewed in the hierarchy of the organization? Will it allow you to get the recognition you require?

11. *Independence.*   Will the job allow you the freedom to plan and organize your time? Is that important to you?

12. *Opportunity for Creativity.*   Will you be able to use your imagination in this position? Can you develop a new way of doing things in your department?

13. *Skill Transferability.*   Are the skills you will develop broad enough to be transferable to other fields? What fields? Do they appeal to you?

(text continues on page 166)

SURVIVING THE JOB SEARCH

The best way to survive the job search is to *organize* it. Schedule your job-search activities on a daily and weekly basis. The following hypothetical schedule should be of some help.

SUNDAY
● Read want-ads in the Sunday employment section of the newspaper in the city in which you want to work. Clip out the want-ads that interest you.

MONDAY
● Write letters in response to want-ads.
● Check in with your counselor at your college placement office. Look at job postings.
● Get names of three alumni in your field of interest.
● Research at least five new companies at your placement library or at a local public library.

TUESDAY
● Write letters to decision-makers at the companies you researched.
● Call alumni contacts and set up interviews for information.
● Read trade publications.

WEDNESDAY
● Interview at ABC Copier Company.
● Write thank-you note to interviewer.
● Call former boss to get additional contacts.
● Have lunch with racquetball partner's contact who works for First National Bank.

THURSDAY
● Follow-up on previous letters sent. Make some appointments.
● Attend lecture at local community college where Ed Sims, Director of Marketing at Itek, is speaking.

(continued on next page)

FRIDAY
- Call your sister's friend for the name and address of her contact at Symtron Industries.
- Write a letter to that contact.
- Go back to the placement office to see if any new jobs have been listed.
- Interview at McGowan Company.
- Write a thank-you letter to interviewer.

SATURDAY
- Relax! You've earned it.

14. *People Management Opportunity.* Will you supervise others? How many people? At what level are they? Is supervision something you like doing?

15. *Asset Management Opportunity.* Will you be controlling equipment or the flow of cash? Do you want this responsibility?

16. *Advancement.* Is advancement locked into a rigid system? What jobs can you move into? Can you transfer into other departments? Will an advanced degree be necessary for promotion?

17. *Image of Company.* Does the reputation of the organization meet your personal and professional needs? Do they produce a product or service you feel good about? Are they an industry leader? Do you care?

18. *Exposure to Outstanding Professionals.* Will you receive exposure to the best minds in your field, or will you be the "big fish in a small pond?" Which do you prefer?

19. *Quality of Management.* Does the company promote and maintain a high quality of managerial talent? Do you prefer working under a strong management team? Do you need a mentor?

20. *Industry.* Is the industry oriented towards growth or stability? How do its salary levels compare to other industries? What are its prospects for the future?

Once you've read the definitions of these 20 factors, go down the list and assign each factor a weight, from one to five. If a factor is not important to you, assign it a '1'. If it is very important to you, assign it a '5'. If it is moderately important, assign it a '3', and so on.

Under the columns labeled "Company Name" (see chart on next page), write in the names and job titles of the offers you're considering. Go down the list once more and decide what company offers more of the factors you consider important. If you're deciding from among three companies, assign a ranking between one and three. If you're deciding between two companies, assign a ranking of one or two. The company where the job factors are most to your liking receives the highest number. Then multiply the weight for each factor by the number assigned to each factor.

Perhaps an example is the best way to explain it. Say you have been

(text continues on page 168)

Job Factors to be Considered	Weights (1 - 5)	Company Name					
		Company A		Company B		Company C	
		Factor Value	Sub Total	Factor Value	Sub Total	Factor Value	Sub Total
1. Location							
2. Good Location for Spouse's Career							
3. Travel							
4. Salary							
5. Benefits							
6. Immediate Use of Training & Experience							
7. Learning Potential							
8. Significant Responsibility							
9. Variety of Work							
10. Job Status							
11. Independence							
12. Opportunity for Creativity							
13. Skill Transferability							
14. People Management Opportunity							
15. Asset Management Opportunity							
16. Advancement							
17. Image of Company							
18. Exposure to Outstanding Professionals							
19. Quality of Management							
20. Industry							
TOTAL:							

offered jobs at two different high-technology companies: Amtron and Tovar. You start deciding where you want to work by considering the *Location,* which you designated as a '3' in importance. Tovar is located in California, and Amtron is located in Texas. You think you'd rather live in California, so you give Tovar a '2' and Amtron a '1', under the heading "Factor Value". Rank the weight times the factor, and Tovar now has a sub-total of '6'. Continue down the list in a similar fashion until you've ranked all 20 factors. Then add up the totals.

Once you've completed this exercise, your choice may be clearer. If your decision surprises you, review your rankings or review the weights you assigned different factors. If you are still surprised, talk to people who can be objective. Many times, all we need to do is express our fears or hesitations aloud, and they become more manageable. An "objective" support group usually does *not* include parents, fellow students, or your spouse. They are too involved in your life. It might include a placement counselor, professor, friends outside school, and professional acquaintances whose opinions you respect.

Finally, make your decision. Think positively. Rest assured you will make the best decision you are capable of making at that time. And remember that no career decision is irreversible.

DEALING WITH REJECTION

First of all, it is important to be aware of the fact that everyone faces rejection in the job search, at every stage along the way. You feel rejected when you send off a resume and no one calls you about it. You feel rejected when you leave a message with an employer's secretary and no one responds. You feel rejected when you go in for an interview and it goes badly. Finally, you feel rejected when you receive a rejection letter.

It happens to everyone, and unfortunately, there is no magic pill to make you feel better when you get rejected. In fact, you feel lousy and it never gets any better. So what can you do about it? Here are some tips:

● *Maintain a proper perspective.* Remember, there are hundreds of jobs you might be interested in, and thousands of companies you could possibly work for. So don't get discouraged over a few rejections. It's just not worth it. Rejection is nothing personal. No one is saying they don't like you, or that you are not a good person. How can they possibly know that in a few short interviews? What they are saying is they have hired someone else instead, and that is their option.

● *Develop a support group.* Many people find it is devastating to handle rejection by themselves. They feel miserable when they are unsuccessful, and this impedes their progress in the job search. If you feel like this, you should probably develop a support group. Seek out people who will listen to you when you are down. Explain to them what you need from them. Is it just a friendly shoulder? Do you want feedback? Do you need reinforcement? Can you find this type of help at home, or among your friends? Is there a group you can join at the counseling center? Talk to your career counselor.

● *Stay active.* Go to seminars and meetings. Introduce yourself to people you want to meet. Ask good questions. Every business and social function you attend is a potential source of information and contacts. You should never leave an event without getting the names of at least two contacts. Set that number as your goal. If you find it difficult to go to events by yourself, ask a friend to accompany you. Explain to them that you need their help.

● *Keep organized.* Set a schedule of regular activities and tentative deadlines for yourself. Determine how many job-search letters you should send out weekly. Make sure you send them. Set goals for yourself. How many interviews should you go on each week? Two? Four? Five? Look at the odds. The more interviews you have, the greater your chance is for success. Make plans to do library research at least one day a week. Spend one morning a week setting up field interviews. Make a weekly appointment to talk to your career counselor for a progress report. The more organized you are, the easier your job search will be. The less time you have to feel depressed, the less depressed you will feel.

● *Maintain complete records.* An effective job search requires well-organized and complete records. You should keep copies of all correspondence. Maintain a list of your contacts. Record the dates and results of your telephone conversations. Know how you plan to follow up. Document important data about specific interviews. Who did you meet with? How did it go? When did you send a follow-up thank-you letter? When will you hear from them?

● *Treat yourself well, both mentally and physically.* Do things you feel good about. If jogging makes you feel good, force yourself to run often. If you like seeing films, budget your money so you can afford to go to a movie a week. It is easy to withdraw into yourself in a stressful period, and it is important that you don't. Interviewers can easily sense a defeated candidate. That is why it is particularly important to take care of yourself. Make sure you look good. Eat well. Exercise with regularity. Attend to spiritual and psychological needs. Keep well-groomed.

● *Continually evaluate your game plan.* As you know by now, the job search is a process. This means it is ongoing and flexible. Therefore, your game plan must be the same. You must continually evaluate the effectiveness of its elements. If you find your letters are not getting a response, figure out why. If you can't be objective, ask for help. If your resume isn't generating interviews, why is that? Have you stressed your accomplishments? Is it well-written and cleanly typed? If your resume is generating interviews but you're not doing well in those interviews, what is the problem? Are you ill-prepared or do you freeze up? Is your manner antagonistic or aren't you enthusiastic enough? Finally, are you doing everything right, but you just aren't getting the breaks? This happens; just remain patient. Eventually things will break for you.

● *Maintain a positive mental attitude.* This is one of the most important things you can do in the job search. The major difference between a successful job-seeker and an unsuccessful one is a difference of attitude. Everyone finds the job search difficult. Most people suffer disappointments and have setbacks. But successful job-seekers don't give up. What differentiates them from the crowd is they continue to persevere in spite of these setbacks. They are survivors. They realize the job search is a game, and that rejection is nothing personal. On the other hand, the "victims" are destroyed at the first sign of rejection. For some, one "no" is all they need. They immediately decide the "real world" is not for them, and they run home and fill out applications for graduate school. For others, it takes two "nos" before they quit. But if you're a survivor, even the third, fourth, fifth, or fifteenth "no" presents no real problem.

After all, you just need one "yes" to be hired. If that sounds too sugar-coated and Pollyanna-like, so be it. Optimism is the name of the game. There is no sweeter victory than winning the job-search game. So join the ranks of successful job-seekers everywhere. Don't quit until you succeed, and succeed you will!

Bibliography

BIBLIOGRAPHY

Many books have been published that deal with different aspects of career choice and job search. No *single* book will provide all the information and techniques you will use to conduct a successful job-search campaign. In addition to utilizing many of the resources of a library, you will need to develop a personal collection of related books. A representative list of some of the most useful books for the job search follows.

GENERAL BOOKS ON THE JOB SEARCH & RELATED SUBJECTS

What Color is Your Parachute? Richard N. Bolles. Ten Speed Press: Berkeley, CA, 1983, revised.

Describes the ineffectiveness of the traditional job search, and presents a comprehensive alternative method, including resume writing and an interviewing technique. Also includes the "Quick Job Hunting Map", which may be useful.

Go Hire Yourself an Employer. Richard K. Irish. Anchor Press: Garden City, NY, 1978, revised.

Outlines in question-and-answer format an assertive approach to job hunting. Reads easily, and is particularly valuable in providing an effective mental posture for the job search.

The Complete Job Search Handbook. Howard Figler. Holt, Rinehart & Winston: New York, NY, 1980.

Described by the author as containing "all the skills you need to get any job and have a good time doing it." A creatively written guide, enjoyable to use and very substantive.

Who's Hiring Who. Richard Lathrop. Ten Speed Press: Berkeley, CA, 1977, revised.

An excellent book on all facets of the job search, with emphasis on identifying unannounced job openings. A most imaginative and creative approach to resume writing with lots of good examples.

HOW TO TARGET A CAREER

Making Vocational Choices: A Theory of Careers. John L. Holland. Prentice-Hall, Inc.: Englewood Cliffs, NJ, 1973.

Contains an excellent source for determining the people environments you would prefer, "The Self-Directed Search." (Holland's theory is the basis of the Strong-Campbell Interest Inventory, as well as much current literature in the career planning field.) The "Occupations Finder" is a somewhat limited classification, but once you arrive at your "people environment code", the "Interviewing for Information" process will uncover many interesting occupations and industries.

Path: A Career Workbook for Liberal Arts Students. Howard E. Figler. Carroll Press: Cranston, RI, 1979.

A detailed method for identifying values, interests, and skills that may relate to career choice. Actual worksheets make this book a handy tool.

Coming Alive from Nine to Five: The Career Search Handbook. Betty N. Michelozzi. Mayfield Publishing Company: Palo Alto, CA, 1980.

A clear and simple group of exercises for determining skills, strengths, and weaknesses. Worksheets are provided. The "Personality Mosaic Exercise" is particularly valuable.

Planning for Career Options. Catalyst Press: New York, NY, 1978.

A self-guidance workbook which is one volume of the "Career Options Series for Undergraduate Women", which has a broad application for all people. Of particular interest is the values exercise entitled "Rating Your Motivations".

HOW TO USE LIBRARY RESEARCH

General Books:

How to Find Information About Companies. Washington Researchers: Washington, DC, 1983.

A source directory that lists the names, addresses, and phone numbers of more than 1500 federal, state, and private offices that collect data on businesses. Listings include government offices, courts, credit reporting firms, information services, trade associations, and labor unions. Also gives advice on the best use of each listing, as well as the names and phone numbers of contact people.

Encyclopedia of Associations. Gale Research Company: Detroit, MI, 1982.

Volume I: "National Organizations of the U.S." A comprehensive source of detailed information concerning non-profit American membership organizations of national scope. More than 15,300 trade associations, professional societies, labor unions, fraternal and patriotic organizations are listed. A typical entry includes name, address, chief official and title, number of members, staff, state and local groups, description, committees, publications, and convention/meeting information.

Volume II: "Geographic and Executive Indexes". Arranged by location; includes association names, addresses, phone numbers, and executives' names.

Volume III: "New Associations and Projects". Provides same information as Volume I on newly-formed associations.

Encyclopedia of Business Information Sources. Gale Research Company: Detroit, MI, 1983.

Volume I is arranged alphabetically, and contains a variety of major business topics with information on statistical and price sources, handbooks and manuals, periodicals, directories, and bibliographies.

Volume II contains materials about international business information. Contents arranged by geographical location.

Guide to American Directories (11th Edition). Bernard Klein, Editor. Klein Publications: New York, NY, 1982.

Provides complete information on directories published in the United States, categorized under industrial, mercantile, and professional headings.

Trade Directories of the World. Croner Publications Inc.: Queens Village, NY, 1983.

A guide to business and trade directories in the United States, Europe, Africa, Asia, and Australia. A typical entry includes title, description of contents, price, and address. A favorite personal entry is the "Directory of 24-Hour Full-Service Auto-Truck Stops of the U.S.", a useful directory if you are driving cross-country for a job interview.

Directory of Directories. Gale Research Company: Detroit, MI, 1983, revised.

Lists a wide range of publications, including commercial and manufacturing directories; general and specialized lists of cultural institutions; directories of individual industries, trades, and professions; rosters of professional and scientific societies. Also includes membership lists of special interest groups of all kinds — political, recreational, and cultural. Contains three sections: Directory Section, Title Index, and Subject Index. A typical entry includes a description, arrangement, indexes, pages, frequency, editor, and price.

College Placement Annual. College Placement Council, Inc.: Bethlehem, PA, annual.

Lists employers and job opportunities with these employers. Includes a handy index that lists companies geographically and by special employment categories or specialties sought. Also listed are employers with summer and foreign employment available. Distributed free-of-charge to college seniors.

Dictionary of Occupational Titles (4th Edition). U.S. Government Printing Office: Washington, DC, 1977 (updated approximately every 10 years).

The definitive resource for describing over 20,000 jobs in the economy. In addition, it groups occupations into a systematic classification based on similarity of functions and qualifications. Also contains a "How to Use the DOT" section, which is generally helpful in deciphering the system.

Occupational Outlook for College Graduates. U.S. Government Printing Office: Washington, DC, semi-annual.

A companion to the DOT (see previous listing); "a guide to career opportunities for which a college degree is, or is becoming, the usual background for employment." Each occupational statement presents information on the nature of work; places of employment; education, skills, and abilities required for entry; employment outlook; and earnings and working conditions.

Everybody's Business: An Almanac, The Irreverent Guide to Corporate America. Edited by Milton Moskowitz, Michael Katz, and Robert Levering. Harper & Row Publishers, Inc.: San Francisco, CA, 1983, revised.

A valuable book, profiling more than 300 major companies. The editors discover how each company is distinctive by exploring company histories, sales and profit figures, reputations, and ownership information, as well as a wealth of other information. It is a bit irreverent, but it is also an insightful look at some of America's largest corporations.

The American Almanac of Jobs and Salaries. John W. Wright. Avon Books: New York, NY, 1983.

An excellent way to find detailed information on occupations, industries, and salaries. This comprehensive look at the world of work provides job descriptions, evaluations of future opportunities, and salary listings, as well as fringe benefits and training requirements for literally hundreds of occupations and professions.

HOW TO USE LIBRARY RESEARCH

Specialized Directories:

A. Business:

Standard & Poor's Register of Corporations, Directors, and Executives. Standard & Poor's, a subsidiary of McGraw-Hill: New York, NY, annual.

An alphabetical list of approximately 38,000 United States and Canadian corporations, with information that includes officers' names, products, standard industrial classification, sales range, and number of employees. The second section gives brief information on about 70,000 executives and directors. An index of companies by SIC industries is at the front.

Billion Dollar Directory: America's Corporate Families. Dun & Bradstreet Inc.: New York, NY, annual.

Identifies major U.S. parent companies and displays corporate family linkage of subsidiaries and divisions. Directory listings include 2600 parent companies in the United States and over 24,000 subsidiary companies. Corporate family listings appear alphabetically, geographically, and by product (Standard Industrial Code) classification.

Dun's Employment Opportunities Directory/The Career Guide. Dun & Bradstreet Inc.: Parsippany, NJ, 1983, annual.

A comprehensive guide to over 4000 companies, including identifying information (names, titles, addresses, and phone numbers); a brief history of the company and its line of business; an overview of career opportunities; and the educational specialties the company hires. The employers are cross-referenced by company name geography, industry classification, and educational discipline sought.

EIS Directory of the Top 1500 Private Companies. Economic Information Systems Inc.: New York, NY, annual.

This directory covers the top privately-held United States companies ranked according to sales. Entries include identifying information, descriptions of products or services, sales volume and type of ownership. Geographic index available.

B. Industry:

Thomas Register of American Manufacturers. Thomas Publishing Company: New York, NY, annual.

Volumes 1-9: "Products and Services" are listed alphabetically. For use in locating the availability and location of specific products or services.

Volumes 10-11: "Company Profiles". For use when you want to learn more about a company and how to contact it. You will find information on more than 115,000 U.S. companies, in alphabetical order, including addresses and phone numbers, asset ratings, company executives, location of sales offices, distributors, plants, or service/engineering offices. Many companies also provide a complete profile of their subsidiaries and divisions and entire product lines, with the information needed to contact these facilities.

Volumes 12-17: "Catalogs of Companies". For use when you need detailed catalog information — specifications, drawings, photos, availability, and performance data.

C. Education & Welfare:

Handbook of Private Schools. Porter Sargent Publishers Inc.: Boston, MA, annual.

Covers more than 1900 elementary and secondary boarding and day schools. Names of administrators included.

Higher Education Exchange. Peterson's Guides, Inc.: Princeton, NJ, 1978.

Covers 3200 colleges, universities, and graduate and professional schools in the United States and Canada; government agencies, professional associations, foundations, and other organizations concerned with higher education; and companies supplying products and services to higher education. Institutions are indexed by geography; companies are classified by product or service.

American Trade Schools Directory. Croner Publications Inc.: Queens Village, NY, 1983, annual.

Includes 8000 private and public trade, industrial, and vocational/technical schools. Arranged geographically.

Directory of Educational Associations. U.S. Department of Health, Education, and Welfare, U.S. Government Printing Office: Washington, DC.

Includes 900 associations related to education, foundations concerned with education, and religious education associations. Names of principal officers and secretaries are listed.

Education Directory: Colleges and Universities and **Education Directory: Public School Systems** and **Education Directory: State Education Agency Officials.** U.S. Department of Education, U.S. Government Printing Office: Washington, DC, annual.

Three separate volumes listing 3100 accredited two- and four-year college level programs, 16,000 operating local public schools, and 1500 principal officers of education agencies. Indexes are alphabetical and geographic.

Public Welfare Directory. American Public Welfare Association: Washington, DC, annual.

Covers federal, state, county, and major city public welfare agencies, including name, address, names of key personnel, and type of service and clientele. Also includes general information about subjects related to public welfare — child support enforcement, probation and parole services, and many others.

National Directory of Private Social Agencies. Social Service Publications, Division of Croner Publications Inc.: Queens Village, NY, 1983, annual.

Lists over 14,000 agencies in the United States by field of services and geographical location. Provides full address and service descriptions for such areas as family and child welfare, vocational services for the handicapped, sheltered workshops, naturalization and legal matters, homemaker services, service institutions (other than hospitals), ethnic and professional groups, and rehabilitation.

D. Arts & Communication:

The Working Press of the Nation. National Research Bureau, Inc.: Chicago, IL, annual.

Volume I: "Newspaper Directory". Contains listings on newspapers, syndicates, news services, newsreels, and photo services. There is also an index of editorial personnel by subject, and an index of newspapers by geography.

Volume II: "Magazine Directory". Lists over 4800 magazines, including consumer, service, trade, and industrial.

Volume III: "TV and Radio Directory". Covers over 8400 radio and TV stations. Detailed information includes power, network affiliation, airtime, and management and programming personnel.

Volume IV: "Feature Writer and Photographer Directory". Lists over 1800 feature writers and photographers, home addresses, subject areas of interest, and publications accepting their works.

Volume V: "Internal Publications". Lists detailed information on the publications of more than 3500 United States companies, government agencies, clubs, and other groups.

Broadcasting Yearbook. Broadcasting Publications, Inc.: Washington, DC, semi-annual.

A comprehensive directory for the broadcasting industry. Divided into six major sections: the television marketplace and national and Canadian TV facilities; a list of AM and FM radio stations in the United States and Canada; directors of advertising agencies, station representatives, and radio and TV commercial production houses; equipment manufacturers and consulting engineers; and consultants in some broadcasting fields and principal trade associations.

Audio/Visual Market Place: A Multimedia Guide. R.R. Bowker Company: New York, NY, 1983, biennial.

A directory of the audio/visual industry, listing producers and distributors, equipment, service and organzations, conventions, film festivals, and others involved in the industry.

Literary Marketplace. R.R. Bowker Company: New York, NY, 1983, annual.

A comprehensive directory of American book publishing. Covers the following publishing and related areas: book publishing, associations, agents and agencies, services and suppliers, direct mail promotion, review, selection, and reference, radio, television, and motion pictures, wholesale, export, and import, bank, manufacturing, magazines, and newspaper publishing.

The National Directory for the Performing Arts and Civic Centers (3rd Edition). John Wiley & Sons: New York, NY, 1978.

Lists organizations in this field, as well as for civic centers and other performing facilities. Information such as the organization's purpose, budget, staff, management, officers, supporting boards, source of income, seasons, and sponsoring groups is provided. Facility information covers type, seating capacity, stage, architect, management, and contacts for rental agreements. Entries are grouped alphabetically, geographically, and by category (dance, theater, etc.). A companion volume, "The National Directory for the Performing Arts/Educational" contains basic information on major schools and institutions that offer training in the performing arts.

E. Health:

Health Organizations of the U.S., Canada, and the World. Gale Research Company: Detroit, MI, 1981.

Covers several hundred professional groups, voluntary associations, foundations, and other organizations concerned with health, medicine, and related fields. A typical entry includes organization name, address, phone, name of principal executive, and description of activities.

National Health Directory, 1983. John T. Grupenhoff, Editor. Aspen Systems Corporation: Rockville, MD, 1983.

Includes 11,500 public officials at policy-making levels concerned with health care services and delivery. Covers federal and state agencies, including personnel of state health planning agencies and health systems agencies. Arranged by level of government and agency.

American Hospital Association Guide to the Health Care Field. American Hospital Association: Chicago, IL, annual.

Offers a wide range of information on 7000 hospitals, more than 29,000 members, and 11,000 health-related organizations. Also includes manufacturers and distributors of hospital and health care products. Arranged geographically and alphabetically.

F. Government & Public Affairs:

United States Government Manual. Office of the Federal Register, U.S. General Services Administration: Washington, DC, annual.

Provides comprehensive information on the agencies of the legislative, judicial, and executive branches, and on quasi-official agencies, international organizations, boards, committees, and commissions. A typical agency description includes a list of principal officials, an organizational chart, a summary statement on the agency's purpose and role, a brief history of the agency, a description of its programs and activities, and a "Sources of Information" section, which is particularly helpful by providing the addresses and telephone numbers for obtaining information on consumer activities, contracts and grants, employment, and publications.

Encyclopedia of Governmental Advisory Organizations. Gale Research Company: Detroit, MI, 1981.

A reference guide to presidential advisory committees, public advisory committees, and other government-related boards, panels, and commissions. Over 3400 committees are included, with information such as name and address, name and title of senior staff member, programs, membership, staff, subsidiary units, and publications and reports.

The National Directory of State Agencies 1982-1983. Information Resources Press: Arlington, VA, 1982.

A valuable resource for identifying state agencies and their areas of responsibility. Contents include an alphabetical list of agency functions, and agencies by state and function. A typical entry includes names of key personnel with address and telephone number.

Working for Consumers — A Directory of State and Local Organizations. Consumer Federation of America: Washington, DC, annual.

Covers 400 consumer organizations, public interest groups, self-help groups, and similar organizations concerned with consumer protection and concerns. A typical entry includes organization name, address, phone number, name of director, and focus of concerns.

The Official U.S. Guide to Leading Positions in the Government: Presidential and Executive Appointments, Salaries, Requirements and Other Vital Statistics for Job Seekers. U.S. Government Printing Office: Washington, DC.

Known in the federal government as "The Plum Book", it covers positions outside the realm of the Civil Service system, the "plum" political appointments. Entries include location and title of position, type of appointment, and salary.

G. Research & Science:

Research Centers Directory (8th Edition). Gale Research Company: Detroit, MI, 1983.

A directory of over 5000 research institutes, centers, foundations, laboratories, bureaus, and other non-profit research facilities in the United States and Canada. It is arranged alphabetically and by field of research, including agriculture, home economics and nutrition; business, economics, and transportation; engineering and technology; government and public affairs. Information includes scope of research activities, names of publications, sources of funding, and names and addresses of principal researchers.

Industrial Research Laboratories of the U.S. (18th Edition). R.R. Bowker Company: New York, NY, 1983.

Information on over 9000 non-governmental research and development laboratories operated primarily by industrial firms. Also includes non-profit or privately-financed firms doing research, development, engineering, consulting, or behavioral research in support of and for industry. A typical listing cites field of research interest and names of key personnel. Contains both subject and geographical indexes.

Peterson's Annual Guide to Engineering, Science, and Computer Jobs. Peterson's Guides, Inc.: Princeton, NJ, annual.

Contains over 800 research, consulting, manufacturing, government, and technical service organizations that hire college and university graduates in technical disciplines. Entries include organization, name, address, contact person, type of organization, number of employees, description of opportunities, starting location, salary and benefits. Convenient indexes include a breakdown by discipline, special interests (e.g., foreign students), geography, and number of employees.

Business Week — R&D Scoreboard Issue. McGraw-Hill Inc.: New York, NY, annual.

Lists more than 600 companies reporting expenditures of $1 million or more annually for research and development. Arranged alphabetically by industry.

Energy Research Programs. Jacques Cattell Press: Tempe, AZ, 1982.

Includes over 6000 companies, non-profit organizations, universities, and government facilities involved in energy production, management and experimentation in the United States, Canada, and Mexico. Lists organization's name and address, names of key executives and research staff, description of research and scientific disciplines represented by the staff. Indexed alphabetically, geographically, and by research subject.

HOW TO WRITE A RESUME

The Perfect Resume. Tom Jackson. Anchor Press: Garden City, NY, 1981.

A workbook with a sense of humor, detailing a step-by-step approach to resume preparation. Provides many good sample resumes and cover letters.

The Resume Workbook. Carolyn F. Nutter. Carroll Press: Cranston, RI, 1978, revised.

As the title suggests, a workbook approach to resume preparation. Provides detailed guidelines for developing a resume. Describes four kinds of resumes, and tells you which situations to use them in. Illustrates one resume done in the four different ways, which offers help by demonstrating how the same information can be used differently.

HOW TO WRITE A COVER LETTER

The Professional Job Changing System. Performance Dynamics, Inc.: Verona, NJ, 1981.

Subtitled "the World's Fastest Way to Get a Better Job". It may not be that, but it does offer some concrete suggestions for conducting an effective job search, primarily for experienced people seeking a career in business. The book's strength for a recent graduate is in the extensive examples of letters it presents. Although the text of the letters may not provide an exact fit for your own background, you will read a valuable way for putting your ideas in writing.

184

HOW TO ORGANIZE A DIRECT CONTACT CAMPAIGN

The National Job Bank. Robert Lang Adams, Senior Editor. Bob Adams Inc.: South Boston, MA, 1983.

The National Job Bank provides comprehensive information on major employers in the nation's 10 key job markets. Individual "Job Bank" books are available for each of these 10 regional job markets, including: The Boston Job Bank, The Greater Chicago Job Bank, The Metropolitan New York Job Bank, The Northern California Job Bank, The Southern California Job Bank, The Pennsylvania Job Bank, The Texas Job Bank, The Metropolitan Washington Job Bank, The Southwest Job Bank, and The Greater Atlanta Job Bank. These books provide geographically segmented listings of business and institutions. They tell you where to write, the phone number to call, and often give personnel contacts and hiring activity information. They are a valuable resource, and will eliminate many hours of research work in developing a list of companies of interest.

The Hidden Job Market for the Eighties. Tom Jackson and Davidyne Mayleas. Time Books: New York, NY, 1981.

The authors claim that 85-90% of the jobs available on any given day exist in the "hidden job market", and they provide you with strategies for locating that market. Theirs is a highly interactive approach containing study sheets and exercises. The main value of this book is in describing the way the labor market works.

HOW TO INTERVIEW

Sweaty Palms: The Neglected Art of Being Interviewed. H. Anthony Medley. Wadsworth Publishing Company, Inc.: Belmont, CA, 1978.

An easy-to-read, anecdotal, humorous, yet very detailed "how to" book. The book covers — sometimes in a bit too much detail for those with some interviewing experience — all the pertinent areas of job interviewing, including types of interviews and preparation tips for them. Also includes valuable sections on dress, salary, and discrimination. Provides concrete, sensible advice.

Your Perfect Right: A Guide to Assertive Living. Robert E. Alberti and Michael L. Emmons. Impact Publishing Company: San Luis Obispo, CA, 1982.

Not strictly designed to improve job interviewing skills, but rather a valuable guide to assertive behavior. Written for the lay person with almost no jargon, the value of this book is in helping you overcome personal powerlessness, and enabling you to act in your own best interest without undue anxiety. Practicing what they preach will aid you immeasurably in job interviews.

Dress for Success and **The Women's Dress for Success Book.** John T. Molloy. Warner Books: New York, NY, 1976 and 1978.

The author considers himself a "wardrobe engineer", and assists you in improving your appearance based on his own scientific research. Again, not a book dealing with job interviewing per se, but because the way you look is so critical to the success of your interviews, these two books have been included in this bibliography. The books are comprehensive and thorough, but may be a bit rigid for some tastes. A chapter on dressing for job interviews is included in each book.

THE NATIONAL JOB BANK

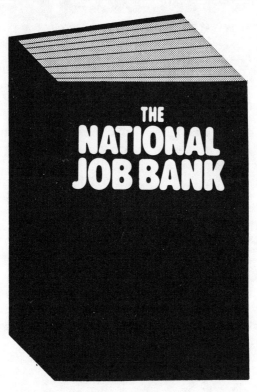

* Contacts and descriptions
  for 10,000 employers.

* 1,600 pages. Hardcover.
  6 x 9.

* Covers: Metro New York, Boston,
  Chicago, D.C./Baltimore, Atlanta,
  Texas, California, Pennsylvania,
  Colorado, Arizona, New Mexico and
  Utah.

* Organized geographically.
  Indexed by industry.

THE NATIONAL JOB BANK

In a single convenient volume, *The National Job Bank* helps job-hunters quickly locate pertinent information on major employers in the nation's ten key job markets.

Each of 10,000 entries includes where to write, the phone number to call, the person to contact to obtain a professional job and a brief description of the firm. Some listings also include typical professional job categories.

The book is organized by the ten key job markets covered. An overall industry cross-index helps pinpoint employers nationwide in any particular field.

The *National Job Bank* is based upon Bob Adams' local *Job Bank* books, which have become local bestsellers, helping tens of thousands find better jobs. Available to libraries for 60 days on approval.

ISBN #0-937860-07-7.
Hardcover only.
Price: $79.95

BOB ADAMS INC.
The Career Guide Specialist
840 Summer St., Boston MA 02127

NEW YORK! BOSTON! CHICAGO! CALIFORNIA! TEXAS! PENNSYLVANIA! WASHINGTON DC/BALTIMORE!

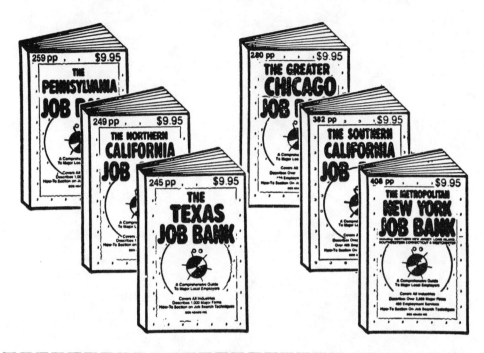